THE REST OF THE WAY

THE REST OF THE WAY

*A Coming Out Story
for Parents and Gay Children*

ENID DUCHIN JACKOWITZ

The Rest Of The Way:
A Coming Out Story for Parents and Gay Children

The Rest Of The Way
P. O. Box 940276
Maitland, FL 32794-0276

Use of lyrics from "You've Got To Be Taught" by permission
Copyright © 1949 by Richard Rodgers and Oscar Hammerstein II
Copyright Renewed
WILLIAMSON MUSIC owner of publication and allied rights throughout the World. International Copyright Secured. All Rights Reserved. Used by Permission

"The Rose" by Amanda McBroom. Copyright © TKTK. International Copyright Secured. All Rights Reserved. Used by Permission.

Lines from "In Whatever Time We Have" by Stephen Schwartz from the musical play *Children of Eden,* © 1991 by Grey Dog Music, are reprinted with permission.

The Kinsey Scale from *Sexual Behavior in the Human Male* by Alfred C. Kinsey, Wardell B. Pomeroy, and Clyde E. Martin (Philadelphia: W. B. Saunders Co., 1948). Copyright © The Kinsey Institute. Reproduced by permission of The Kinsey Institute for Research in Sex, Gender, and Reproduction, Inc.

Cover designed by Jake Stevens

First Edition

THE LIBRARY OF CONGRESS HAS CATALOGUED THIS BOOK AS FOLLOWS:
2009905981

ISBN: 1-4392-4603-3
ISBN 13: 9781439246030

BookSurge Publishing
7290 Investment Drive
Charleston, SC 29418
www.amazon.com
1-866-308-6235

Printed in the United States of America

With all my love, this book is dedicated to my husband Syd for being with me every step of the way—since the day we met. It's been like jelly baby...

And to my two precious granddaughters, so that one day they will know the story.

CONTENTS

PREFACE

I will never forget the night...the night my son first told my husband and me he was gay. As distraught as I was, I remember having a flash of insight, though it didn't last long, that somehow I would come through this time of upheaval with a deeper understanding and love of my son. It would take many years for that to happen, but eventually it became a reality.

For the longest time I was filled with grief and shame, and unable to accept my son. When the day finally came and the struggle was behind me, I knew I could help other parents going through this often difficult journey. Over the years I toyed with the idea of writing a book about my coming-out experience. I had visions of sitting down at my computer and writing my story from beginning to end with ease. Not quite. Writing a book, I soon discovered, was a lot harder than I had ever imagined—especially one as personal as this. I started writing parts of the book dozens of times but became discouraged and daunted by the task and would put it aside, working on it only intermittently. It was a little like running on a treadmill and going nowhere fast.

Then I heard from Brian, one of my son's oldest and dearest gay friends. Devastated, he called me after coming out to his parents. They told him they would never accept him being gay. As far as they were concerned they wanted no part of this Brian—the gay Brian. In spite of their disapproval and judgment, Brian knew his parents loved him and that his news couldn't be easy for them to accept. But what he hadn't expected was how ashamed they were of him. He wondered if he could remain the confident, self-assured man he had always been when his own parents treated him as a disgrace and an embarrassment. He longed for his parents to understand that he was born gay, that he hadn't chosen it. But as far as they were concerned he made the choice to become gay, for what reason they couldn't fathom.

No matter how many times Brian told his parents he wasn't interested in finding the "right" girl, there continued to be desperate attempts by them to find *her*, so he could live what they saw as a "normal" life. For them that meant getting married and having children. But what would have been normal for Brian was the freedom and acceptance to live his life "out and proud" as a gay man.

Brian needed some advice on how to handle the situation. He sent me a copy of the letter he wrote to his parents wanting my perspective. It was heartbreaking on many levels. "What do I have to do?" Brian asked his parents. "Live a lie and deny the truth about myself to keep you happy? Do you think I owe you that? Why can't we be real with each other?

Am I supposed to be a 'Yes' son who only tells you what you want to hear? If we can't talk about issues regarding my sexual orientation, an integral part of my being, then what kind of a relationship will we have?"

Why was it so hard for Brian's parents, and for so many other parents, to understand and accept their gay child? Why indeed? A complicated question.

Reading Brian's letter brought me back to my son's coming out and how similarly to Brian's parents my husband and I had reacted; it was the way so many parents react. In many ways Brian's parent's story was like my own and I couldn't help but recognize the universality of it. It wasn't hard to imagine how many families experienced a version of that story after hearing the words "I'm gay" from their child. I felt compelled to do something to change the way those families thought about homosexuality, to help them have greater understanding and compassion, so that they too might go the rest of the way back to their child. I became more determined than ever to finish the book.

It is my sincerest hope that this book will be read by those with a gay family member and that they will find some understanding and comfort in these pages recounting my journey. And most importantly, that they will find a place of acceptance for their child, as my family did, and as Brian's family eventually did as well.

THE REST OF THE WAY

There was once a king who had a major disagreement with his son. The son, feeling angry and misunderstood, gathered his belongings and departed his father's kingdom. The son traveled far away from his father and settled in a distant kingdom, where he lived his life. After many years had passed, the king, missing his son greatly, sent word for his son to come home. Although time had healed some of the pain, the son could not bring himself to return to his father's kingdom. So he sent word that he would not come because it was too far to travel. The king sent this reply to his son: "Then come as far as you can, and I will meet you the rest of the way."[1]

This book is about meeting my older son the rest of the way. To get there I had to travel a road filled with fear at every turn. But I knew it was a road I had to take—one of my beloved sons was at the other end. And so I did. This is the story of that journey.

---

[1] From a Talmudic story.

CHAPTER 1

LIFE-CHANGING

Before we can move into a new arrangement,
we must first go through a period of de-rangement.
(M.C. Richards)

❧

Children of the fifties, my husband, Syd, and I grew up in a time when things were a whole lot simpler than they are today. We met in high school in study hall when Syd was a senior and I was a sophomore. That day I went home from school and told my mother, "I met the boy I'm going to marry today, mom." I was sixteen years old and could barely decide what outfit to wear to school, but when I met Syd, I was certain he was the one. I didn't have to think, or question. I knew. I've never been so sure of anything in my life. Though my mother dismissed my declaration of love as yet another infatuation in a long line of infatuations, there was no doubt in my mind that one day Syd and I would be together. During study hall we did little studying. Instead we told jokes and sent notes back and forth to each other. When I got a pass to the library, Syd would meet me there. One day he said, "Let's sneak out of school and go for coffee." I wouldn't have dared to go alone and thought he was so cool. Furtively, we drove off to a local coffee shop, hoping we wouldn't get caught. Getting back to school just in time for the bell to ring, we felt like we pulled off a coup. So it went for the rest of the semester and has continued for over fifty years.

We went together from that time on, and after Syd graduated from college, we married and had two children, Michael and Howard. We moved to Maitland, a suburb of Orlando, when Syd went to work at Walt Disney World's Legal Department in 1973. From the beginning, Syd and I were deeply connected to each other and later to our sons. They were caring, bright, fun-loving, and creative. Where we went, they went—to movies, the theater, restaurants, and on vacations.

We thought ours was a 'perfect' family until one night in June of 1986, when everything fell apart. Our oldest son came into the family room, sat down and said nervously, "There's something I have to tell you." Michael was twenty-one years old and about to enter medical school in the fall. Weeks before, when we were in Atlanta for his college graduation, I had sensed that something wasn't right, but couldn't put my finger on it. I didn't ask Michael if anything was wrong then, I suppose, because something told me not to; now I was about to find out what it was. Michael was tense and extremely anxious, and a feeling of dread settled about me like an icy chill. Sitting on the sofa, as Michael began, I felt my breath stop, as though all the air in the room suddenly disappeared. It's funny how we remember that moment—Syd in his way, me in mine. Syd thought Michael was about to tell us he was getting engaged, but based on Michael's nervousness, he wondered if his girlfriend was pregnant. No, that wasn't it.

"This is so hard for me," Michael said hesitantly. "And I know how hard it will be for you. Even so, it's something you have to know." After a deep breath, he continued, "I've been unsure of my sexuality and struggling with this for a long time. It isn't something I would have chosen, but after agonizing and soul searching, I can't deny it any more; I'm gay." There it was. In a moment, everything changed, and I knew our lives would never be the same.

Here sat my son, my handsome, outgoing, well-rounded son, who seemed to have everything going for him, telling us he was gay. It didn't compute. Michael had been an excellent student, involved in school activities, achieving awards and accolades. In high school he dated, and there were always girls around the house. In college he had met a wonderful girl; they had been going together for about a year and it looked serious. Nothing suggested he was anything other than straight. If there were clues, we didn't see them.

Later Michael said he grappled with whether or not to tell us. Friends warned him of what could happen when delivering this news: getting kicked out of the house, being cut off financially, even total estrangement. Though Michael knew there was a lot to lose, we were his family and he took the risk, believing in time we'd come to accept him as he was.

But once I heard the word "gay," I had a hard time listening. Michael's words came to me filtered through my prejudice and yes, my homophobia, a word I didn't know, but one I was about to become very familiar with. I tried to wrap my brain around what he was saying, but everything seemed to be moving in slow motion. I gave no thought to what Michael must have gone through or how daunting this disclosure must be for him; all I could think about was what this meant to us and our family.

Michael's news came in 1986 when there was no *Ellen,* no *Will & Grace.* AIDS was rampant and people like us were terrified of what was called the "gay disease." I was a housewife then, and knew little about homosexuality; what I did know was tinged with prejudice and half-truths. Later I would learn that in 1973 the *DSM-III* (*Diagnostic and Statistical Manual of Mental Disorders*), published by the American Psychiatric Association (APA), had removed homosexuality as a disorder from its pages. But the understanding that being gay was not abnormal or deviant has not been so easily removed from the minds of some of society. With the Stonewall riots in 1969, the declassification of homosexuality in the DSM, and the election of Harvey Milk to San Francisco's Board of Supervisors, the burgeoning gay rights movement took off going full swing. It was met with protests and demonstrations from anti-gay rights activists. How well I remember Anita Bryant spearheading the movement in Florida. But being a stay-at-home mom at the time, I didn't pay much attention to what I saw as her anti-gay ranting.

Now all I knew was my son was gay and I was stunned by the news. Syd and I began a litany of questions and recriminations. How could he be sure?

Maybe it was just a stage he was going through. What about all of his girlfriends? Was it something we did? I did? What could we do to fix it? How could he just throw away our family's values and beliefs so casually, and discard them for a gay lifestyle? This wasn't how we had raised him. Then how could it have happened? We wondered. Why did he need to tell us? Did he think we would just accept it? What was he thinking? *Was* he thinking? It didn't compute. The situation didn't make sense; it felt like I was looking at a ship in a bottle. I had no idea how it got in there in the first place, or how to get it out.

Michael tried to assure us that it wasn't a choice, but we weren't hearing him. We just didn't get it. I knew precious little about homosexuality and had always assumed people "turned" gay because of bad parenting, the wrong kind of friends, or being exposed to other gay people. That's where I was coming from. The questions that were rushing through my head were like a relentless freight train. I carried them around like pieces of luggage to be guarded, not trusting myself to set them down. Answers were nowhere to be found.

Even though we both were overwhelmed by Michael's news, Syd remained loving toward Michael, but I began to distance myself from him. I felt such a sense of shame, believing he was disgracing himself and our family that I could barely look at him. He was living at home that summer before starting medical school, and I counted the days until he would leave.

It seemed impossible that this could have happened to our family. Our children, prized above all else, were our whole world. We made sacrifices for them so they could have the best of everything, and what we expected in return was to bask in the pleasure of their accomplishments: college graduations, grad school, marriage, and grandchildren. Above all, we anticipated being doting grandparents. Michael's news broke this unspoken covenant, and all of our dreams for him and for us seemed to vanish, blown away like a pile of dead leaves. How this was possible was beyond my comprehension. Shattered, I wondered if our lives would ever be whole again.

My self-esteem plummeted and I began a downward spiral into a deep depression. I believed my one worthwhile accomplishment was raising decent, loving children. Had I failed even at that? I didn't want to eat, couldn't sleep; I could find no place for myself. The thought of how people would react hung over me like an unwelcome visitor about to come calling.

Discovering your child is gay, especially with no suspicion, can turn life upside down. At least it did for the two of us. It would take time before we began inching our way out of the closet we found ourselves trapped in.

The door Michael flung open was one I would not have unlocked, let alone opened, but there it was and I knew at some point I would have to go through it and see what was on the other side.

CHAPTER 2

UPHEAVAL

"We do not see things as they are.
We see them as we are."
(A Talmudic Teaching)

❧

That summer, as the weeks went by, our family life deteriorated. Syd and I rationalized that our younger son Howard didn't need to know about Michael, at least until we figured things out. So we kept the news from him. This would be the first in a long line of secrets. In his teens and caught up in his own life, Howard may not have been sure of what was happening at the time, but like the rest of us, he couldn't avoid feeling the chaos swirling around what had been our once peaceful home. I avoided Michael and had as little contact with him as necessary. Then one evening he announced, matter-of-factly, that he planned to tell some friends at the Jewish Community Center (JCC) where he worked that he was gay. I was floored.

"How could you even think of doing such a thing?" I asked.

"I'm gay." Michael said. "That's the reality. Sooner or later it will come out."

Please God, let it be later, I silently prayed. I was still hoping for a miracle living in the "if only's," desperately hoping Michael would wake up and be "normal."

"What do you think will happen if they find out at the J?" I asked. "You're sure to be fired. No one will trust you around young children."

As I spoke the words, I knew they had no validity, yet out they tumbled. Michael's only interest in children was that he wanted to be a parent one day. I knew that yesterday. How could I doubt it today? What was my doubt about and where did it come from? It was internalized homophobia.[2]

Homophobia was something I had never paid attention to; I don't even think I knew the word, but then suddenly, it was everywhere. Not a day went by without hearing slurs or distasteful jokes against gays and lesbians, words like "queer," "faggot," or the Yiddish slur *"fagele"* echoing in my ears. I pretended not to hear, but the emotional impact of it was crushing. It reminded me of when my grandmother died when I was twelve years old. Before her death I don't remember ever seeing a funeral parlor, but after her death, I saw funeral parlors wherever I went. They seemed to be on every corner. That's how it was with homophobia. One evening we were out to dinner

---

[2] Internalized homophobia is the fear and sometimes hatred of people who are seen as gay, lesbian, or bisexual. Because we've all been brought up in a homophobic society, there are ways we have internalized, consciously or unconsciously, those subtle and not-so-subtle messages of inferiority or otherness.

with a business associate of Syd's who, seeing that our waiter was effeminate, remarked, "They may all be queer as three-dollar bills, but they do make good waiters." I didn't have the courage to say anything; instead I played with the food on my plate, longing for the evening to be over. Yesterday, Michael was a respectable member of the community, today he was not. Today he was "queer as a three-dollar bill." I felt too vulnerable to protect myself, so how could I protect my son from that kind of hurt? I couldn't.

Worry was my constant companion. Syd and I were terrified about AIDS. It was rife in the gay community at that time and the impact of it was overwhelming. Every day seemed to bring news of someone dying from AIDS. We didn't know if Michael was sexually active, but hoped if he was he was using protection. I worried how Howard would feel, what our other relatives' reactions would be, and that it was somehow my fault. Had I done something to cause it? I knew it wasn't anything Syd had done. He was the most loving father. And if it wasn't Syd's fault, it had to be someone's fault, didn't it? I thought it must be mine. Added to this toxic brew was my dread of anyone finding out, which left me trapped in a cycle of depression, fear and shame. How would I ever get free of it? I couldn't think of a way.

Michael gave me a book to read he thought would be helpful, but it treated the coming out period for parents as no big deal. I read the first chapter about parents experiencing conflicting emotions over the news. The message was, "Shake it off and get over it." That was that. So there was no help there. Filled with so many unanswered questions, so much confusion, and much grieving to do, I was so not ready to shake it off. The book remained languishing in the back of my dresser drawer.

When Michael was growing up, he had been the type of kid who loved to conquer new things. If something was a challenge he was ready for it. He learned the guitar, taught himself to play the piano, and even found a way to make statistics enjoyable, getting an A in the process. Was this his next challenge, I wondered? But, why would he be drawn to a gay lifestyle? In my mind being gay meant being lonely and uncommitted—on the fringe, living a deviant life of promiscuity, going to sleazy gay bars, and being seen by society as a pariah. I couldn't understand why my son would choose such a life.

I began slipping deeper into depression, barely functioning. How I wished I could retreat like a turtle and simple disappear into my shell. Syd was able to throw himself into his work, but I could think of little else beside my sorrow and disappointment. Each morning Syd and I took a forty-minute walk, talking, trying to figure things out—with little luck. We felt so adrift, so alone in our pain. I didn't realize it at the time—all I knew then was that my world was falling apart—but looking back, I see that I had always defined my own identity as a wife and mother by who my husband was, and who my sons were, and would become. The picture I had in my mind of homosexuality was one that had been painted by my family and by the world around me—being gay was deplorable, something that would never happen in a good family.

I don't know how I would have survived that time without Syd's love and support. Throughout our marriage, our relationship had always been a top priority for the two of us, but never more than now. Even before Michael's "coming out" day, through the years when Syd was Director of the Legal Department at Walt Disney World, no matter how busy he was, when the kids or I called, he always took time out for us. But adversity is tricky; it either draws people closer or pulls them apart. Gratefully, we became closer, but still unable to make sense of our situation.

I was in such a fog, I didn't know when, but at some point Michael told Howard he was gay. Howard seemed to be okay with it and was especially patient and loving to me during that incredibly difficult time. But he was concerned as he saw our family life disintegrating, and suggested that Syd and I see a counselor. Counseling had never crossed our minds, but he was right. What we were experiencing was such an avalanche of feelings that, of course, we needed help dealing with it.

I remembered meeting an amazing woman a few years earlier, Hedy Schleiffer, a therapist with a reputation for being non-judgmental, open, and accepting. I thought if anyone could help us it was Hedy and I told Syd about her. I was in such a state I couldn't even call to make the appointment for the two of us to see her; so Syd did. Michael went to see Hedy that summer as well, but without Syd and me. It would have been counter-productive for the three of us to go together. What Syd and I needed was a safe place to talk openly about what we were feeling.

The same was true for Michael. When Syd and I arrived at Hedy's office, I was anxious and fearful, but she put us both at ease. While Syd told our story, I sat weeping, a total mess. After a few sessions together I began seeing Hedy alone.

Going to therapy had not even been on my radar screen, but Michael's coming out turned my life into such chaos I knew, if I didn't do something, I would have a complete meltdown. What went on in therapy, what was it about, what would I find? I had no idea and it scared the hell out of me. But therapy turned out to be a godsend. It gave me a place to be heard and understood by someone other than Syd, if just for one hour a week, and most importantly, it gave me a safe place to grieve. The grieving seemed to wash over me in gigantic waves. I grieved that there would be no wedding, no daughter-in-law, no grandchildren—nothing to look forward to. Now I believed there would be only pain and shame from my beloved son who had held such promise. It seemed like our entire family had suddenly gone from respectable to persona non grata. In the time it took to make a cup of tea, I found myself steeped in the shame of having a child who was the member of such an undesirable and often hated group.

Most of the time I hid in my house, crying and ruminating, hoping against hope that this was just a phase, that Michael had taken the wrong road, and that eventually he'd come to his senses. Whenever I went out into the world, I did the best I could to appear as if everything was fine, but inside I felt like I was going the wrong way down a one-way street. The only thing I looked forward to were my weekly therapy sessions with Hedy, who listened to me in a way I had never been listened to before, empathically and non-judgmentally. Her loving acceptance and deep sensitivity created the safety for me to be where I was, with no need to justify any of it. I could just feel whatever I was feeling. Everything spilled out of me—the weeping, the shame, the fear, the pain...and I felt I would drown from the grief of it. Later I wrote a Haiku about this time:

<u>Open the Door</u>

Let Grief be a door
on the river of your tears
and you will not drown.

As the shock of Michael's news began wearing off, I found that under my sadness was a great deal of anger. Because I saw Michael as the cause of my pain, that anger was directed at him. We had terrible rows that ended with me wanting him out of the house and Michael eager for the day he could leave. A low point was when Michael, getting ready to leave for school, told me he wanted to keep kosher. "Why bother," I said. Then added with biting sarcasm, "how can you call yourself a Jew?" Michael was sickened by my words. There was such a wall between us. I was convinced it was too high and too hard to ever get past.

In therapy with Hedy, one day she asked me if I had any gay relatives. I thought of a gay cousin by marriage—not really a cousin but part of our *Mishpucha* (extended family) and how Sonny was treated, kindly, but with little respect. He had, after all, "broken the rules." Being gay was not something that was tolerated in a nice Jewish family. That he was gay was considered a *shunda* (disgrace) and his parents were pitied. The story that was told about Sonny was that he had been crazy in love with a woman, but when she left him and married someone else, that did it. He couldn't handle her rejection, and became gay. Once my mother told me in hushed tones that Sonny wore make-up, which seemed to emphasize his strangeness. I had always liked Sonny and never felt I was prejudiced against him—or anyone else for that matter. But no matter how accepting and tolerant you are when it comes to others, when it's your child who is suddenly openly gay, it's a very different story.

As I explored my life, painfully I realized that somewhere along the way, I had lost myself, and didn't know who I was. What I did know was what mask to wear and what I had to do to get the love I needed from my family. My life, it seemed, had been spent garnering the good opinion of others and letting other people define me. A people pleaser *par excellence,* I did my best to be all things to all people. The only person I didn't know how to please or take care of was myself.

Growing up, I learned not to make waves, to blend in, and like Woody Allen in the movie *Zelig,* I became an accomplished chameleon. When things started to get out of balance during my childhood, I would quickly take my family's emotional temperature and make the needed adjustment to equalize the situation. If humor was needed, I was funny. If the subject needed changing, I changed it. If someone needed their hand held, I held it. I was the proverbial good girl, and did what was expected of me. For the life of me I couldn't understand why Michael refused to do what was expected of him. He knew there was no place in our family landscape for a gay son. So why was he coming out of the closet instead of staying inside of it? I tried to understand and make peace with my disappointment and grief, but no matter how I looked at it, I could not understand how or why this had happened.

Finally, the summer ended and Michael left for school. What a relief. His visits home were only occasional, mostly to see Hedy from time to time. Her acceptance and understanding gave Michael hope that things would get better with time. During those brief weekends we talked about inconsequential things, not the real issues; they were conveniently brushed aside.

In therapy, before long I became aware that the person I was learning about wasn't Michael. It was me.

CHAPTER 3

PICKING UP THE PIECES

Be like the bird that,
passing on her flight
awhile on boughs too slight,
feels them give way beneath her,
and yet sings, knowing that she hath wings.
(Victor Hugo)

∾

I had seen Hedy for a few sessions when she remarked that she never saw anyone dive into the pain the way I did; it was the way she dealt with it, too, she said. How could anyone do otherwise, I wondered? Later I would learn how many people did do otherwise. Some people are thinkers and some are feelers; I was the latter, and all of my life have lived very much in my feelings, so there was little I could do to avoid them.

In therapy, the saying goes, the only way out of the pain is through the pain. The thought of taking a perilous journey into such uncertainty is not what I'd call inviting. But I knew I needed to make the trip, if I wanted to get to the other side. Some time later, I heard a story that I think helps to explain this journey.

"The Lion's Roar" tells of lions hunting their prey. The old lions look ferocious and roar fiercely, but have no teeth or claws and can no longer hunt. In pursuit of food, these old lions go to one side of a field while the young, agile hunter lions go to the other. When a wildebeest comes along, the old lions roar savagely and look ferocious. And the wildebeest, thinking it is escaping, runs in the other direction—but instead of escaping, it runs right into the jaws of the hunter lions. The irony is that had the wildebeest run toward the roar, it would have been safe. Running from our fears and emotions, we often die uncounted deaths, instead of going into the pain and feeling whatever we need to feel by being entirely present to it.

At this time I was still grieving, and through my grief was slowly beginning to purge myself of the sorrow and depression I had been feeling. It was as though I was cleaning out a filing cabinet, filled with other people's beliefs that I somehow had accumulated and filed away as my own. Piece by piece I began tossing out clutter left there by others that didn't belong to me.

I began finding out about unconscious patterns, like being a "people pleaser," that I had learned as a child in order to survive in my family of origin. Sure, being a pleaser helped me get through my childhood, but in the process I had become disconnected from my inherent wholeness, believing I was lovable only when I was doing for others.

Here's an example: when Syd and I and our sons moved to Orlando in 1973, that first year we had company almost every weekend. Not only didn't I know how to say "no" to endless entertaining; I didn't even know I had the right. Syd was working in the legal department at Disney World and had a pass into the Magic Kingdom; it was, we discovered, quite a big drawing card. If all roads led to Rome, for us all avenues led to Orlando. At first I enjoyed having friends and relatives visit. But before long it felt like I was running a hotel, with all the cooking, cleaning, and entertaining, not to mention the laundry. That would have been enough, but each weekend we would *schlep* (drag) our guests to Disney World, get them into the Magic Kingdom and like tour guides accompany them through the park. Syd and I went on the ride "It's a Small World" so many times, we used to count how many dolls were there. When our guests left, it took me the rest of the week to recuperate and get ready for the next round. I was, in the words of Melody Beattie, author of *Codependent No More*, doing all the right things for all the wrong reasons. Years later when I finally found my voice, I went overboard in the opposite direction, saying "no more company at all." That's the way that usually works—like a swinging pendulum, from one extreme to the other, until I was able to find a place of balance in myself.

Each week in therapy, blurred parts of my life came more sharply into focus, and I began to see things through a clearer lens. I had been raised to always put other people's needs first, and believed that anything else was selfish. How liberating to understand that taking care of my own needs meant accepting responsibility for my life and that that was not selfish. It was being respectful and accountable to myself. So when a family member berated me for being selfish, I didn't accept the guilt she tried to deliver, but realized what her anger was really about: I wasn't doing something she wanted me to do.

As I began to set boundaries, there were people in my life who were floored by my new assertive behavior. When Hurricane Floyd was headed our way, reports were that it was expected to cross over the state and hit Orlando that evening. It looked like a monster storm, and weather reports were predicting that even if it moved offshore we could get winds from seventy-five to one hundred twenty-five miles an hour. In preparation Syd and I were busy cleaning up outside when the phone rang. It was a relative of Syd's.

"How are you?" he asked.

Thinking he was calling to see how were doing with the oncoming storm, I said, "We're okay, but very anxious about the hurricane."

"With the problems I'm having, a hurricane is the last thing on my mind," was Syd's relative's less than concerned response. "I need to talk to Syd."

"He can't come to the phone right now," I said, and told him Syd was on a ladder, trimming some limbs from one of our large oak trees.

"What do you mean?" Syd's relative questioned me. In the past I would have interrupted whatever Syd was doing and given him the phone.

"The hurricane may be the last thing on your mind," I said. "But it's the first thing on ours. Syd will have to call you back."

Syd's relative was not a bit happy with my response, and not used to this kind of reaction—not from me. Truthfully, it brought up a flood of feelings, but I stood my ground.

Later he said to me, "I liked you a lot better the way you were before."

A classic line. Of course he did. Before, I did whatever it took, even if it meant letting my house blow away to keep people happy. Everybody liked me better before—everybody but me. Before I was pleasing and pleasant and didn't make waves. I went along, any way the wind blew. Waves were for other people. God forbid, I should say something someone might not like. Now that I'm a therapist, I often tell clients: be mindful when setting boundaries because one thing you can be sure of is family members and friends won't like it. More often than not they'll turn up the heat trying to get things back to the status quo.

Twenty-two years ago, I was content with the accomplishments of my husband and children. I thought I knew who I was and what was important to me. But I didn't have a clue. I was sleepwalking through my life, not living, merely surviving in what I now call a coma consciousness. The thing about waking up is, it isn't easy—not for anyone. A story I heard some years ago explains it very well.

Dave was part of a platoon just beginning basic training. The first morning the bugle sounded at 4:30am and the soldiers were ordered to be lined up, standing at attention for roll call at 5:00am. It was a struggle for all the guys to get up at that hour, particularly Dave, who was a very heavy sleeper.

The first morning Dave tried, but couldn't seem to rouse himself at that frightful hour, so fifteen minutes before roll call a group of the guys in his barracks shook him.

"Dave," they said, "you'd better get up."

But Dave missed roll call, and the whole platoon had to take a lap around the two-mile field.

The next morning, again Dave couldn't seem to wake up, so some of the guys threw him out of bed and doused him with water. Again Dave missed roll call. This time the men in his platoon took two laps around the field.

The third morning, fed up, the entire platoon pulled Dave out of bed, beat the crap out of him, and dragged him outside to roll call.

Sometimes this is what happens to us. The universe sends us a gentle message at first, telling us to *WAKE UP*. If we ignore it, the next message is not so kind. Subsequent messages are stronger and progressively harsher. Sometimes, like Dave, we can't seem to rouse ourselves from unconsciousness until we get the crap kicked out of us.

Here's a poem I wrote that shows how, like Rip Van Winkle, at last I was finally waking from my coma consciousness.

Once, others extolled the symmetry of my life
nice, predictable, consistent
like a Pillsbury biscuit,
looked good
and no dirty bowls.
Until
I made my own recipe
from scratch.
The real thing.
And one thing
about making the real thing,
Sister
that can make one hell of a mess.

CHAPTER 4

A NEW FOUNDATION

*Change and growth take place
when a person has risked himself
and dares to become involved
with experimenting with his own life.*
(Herbert Otto)

༠

During the time I was barely keeping myself afloat, I ran into a friend who could hardly wait to tell me the juicy gossip of the day. "Rumors," Sheila said "are flying. This you won't believe."

But I wasn't a bit interested in hearing her big news and wished I could just disappear. Instead I listened with one ear as she chattered on, waiting for her tale of *loshon hora* (gossiping in a derogatory or harmful way) to be over. I began paying attention when I heard her say ... " a highly respected, unmarried Jewish man... from such a prominent family was—of all things—gay." I was listening with both ears now.

"His family are denying it," Sheila said, "But look at the facts, he's thirty something, hasn't been involved in a serious relationship for years, and isn't interested in meeting any women. People are putting two and two together." Obviously what they were getting wasn't four.

"I tried to fix him up with my cousin last year," Sheila continued. "No wonder he never called her back. Can you imagine, all this time he was nothing more than a *fagele!*"

Just a few months earlier the man in question had been honored as Teacher of the Year. Now, based purely on conjecture that he might be gay, he was ostracized, and talked about in conspiratorial whispers, behind his back. Did the gossip have any basis in fact? I didn't know. But it didn't matter. His parents, once venerated pillars of the Jewish community, took a tumble and were pitied. Nothing trumped being gay.

In the Jewish community anyone gay was considered to be a *shunda*. Even the mention of the word gay brought forth Tsk, Tsk's and snickering. And it was widely accepted that the cause of why someone was gay had a lot to do with the way they were parented. The stereotype of the domineering mother, and the absent, passive father was—and, in fact still is—prevalent in some circles.

As I listened to this story unfolding, what I knew as sure as I knew my own name was that if word got out that Michael was gay, my family would be treated no differently than this family. Having gay gossip was akin to throwing raw meat into a lion's den. It would be torn apart and devoured. The only way I felt I could protect my family from being on the receiving end of such unwanted scorn or ridicule was to continue pretending everything was "perfect" in my life instead of in complete shambles. Anyone taking a look would have seen me in a perfectly manicured garden, brimming with flowers, in reality my garden was overflowing with weeds.

In her book, *Goodbye, I Love You*, Carol Lynn Pearson said, "Dogma collides with reality when the people involved are those you love, suddenly you see with different eyes." It was so true. Not only was I seeing things differently, I was hearing things I never heard before—at least not consciously. My friends, whom I thought of as open-minded and tolerant, were, I found, quite the opposite. Though they were unaware that Michael was gay, and never would have said such things to my face, nevertheless, there I was inadvertently on the receiving end of their insensitive, prejudiced gossip. It finally reached a point where I couldn't ignore my friends' comments anymore. That, compounded by the fact that I didn't feel safe enough to tell them about Michael, meant it was time for a change. I needed to meet new people, people who were tolerant and open-minded.

For me to do that meant I'd have to make a lot of changes. I had grown up in a world filled with judgment and self-righteousness. Seeing what that does to people, what it did to me, I knew the most important change would be to find a way to be less judgmental and more tolerant myself. This was no small task, since I could see the prejudice in everyone around me, but ironically, I couldn't see it in myself. What a rude awakening that was.

At this point I was no longer in therapy and knew if I wanted to find my way out of the box I was in it was time to start stretching. I saw a flyer for a two-day workshop given by the Foundation for Mideast Communication (FMC), a group Hedy was involved in. FMC promoted face-to-face communication between Israelis and Palestinians in the Middle East as well as among Christians, Jews, and Muslims throughout the United States and Canada. I decided to take a risk and go. My sister, brother-in-law and nephews lived in Jerusalem, and I thought the workshop might be a good way for me to move past my narrow way of understanding the situation there. Since I had never even met an Arab person before, it was way out of my comfort zone; I did it anyway.

Going to that workshop, led by Hedy, her husband Yumi, and Michael Lame, founder of FMC, was a major turning point in my life. During that first day, there was disagreement and a good deal of conflict; I wondered what were we accomplishing. If we, as a group of Arabs, Christians, and Jews sitting in a room in Orlando, couldn't agree and find a place of resolution, how could we expect the people living in the conflict on the other side of the world to do so? It seemed there was only one place we were in agreement: all of us were overwhelmed and felt a sense of hopelessness that the situation could change. But, as the day went on and people began telling their stories of how they had been affected personally by the conflict, something shifted in me.

After Yumi, who is a Holocaust survivor, spoke about losing his family during that nightmarish time, a young Palestinian man got up from the table, approached Yumi, and with tears in his eyes apologized for the pain Yumi had endured. The Palestinian man didn't take responsibility or blame for what happened. The Holocaust took place years before he was born, but he understood, probably for the first time, the enormity of pain the man on the other side of the room had suffered. As the day went on, a Palestinian man who had lost his home spoke about his despair and helplessness at being displaced, living in a refugee camp, under the most primitive circumstances. As we continued around the circle, I realized that before there could be a change in people's position, what had to change were the perceptions each of us held. Maybe we weren't changing anything in the Middle East, but my perceptions were certainly changing. Longfellow said, "If we could read the secret history of our enemies, we should find in each person's life sorrow and suffering enough to disarm all hostility." So it did, in my heart, as I opened to the pain and suffering on both sides, something I had not considered before.

At the end of the workshop, Hedy asked if anyone would like to join FMC's Orlando Board of Directors. I had come to a crossroads, and knew it was time to take another path to explore new ways of understanding myself and the people around me. My hand shot up. It was way out of the box for me. I wanted these open-minded, vibrant, genuine people in my life and was so ready to make a change. The seeds that were planted that weekend enlarged my view of the world, and cultivated acceptance and respect in me for people from different backgrounds and environments.

I wish I could say my tolerance spilled over to Michael; it didn't—yet. I was still a long way from being comfortable with the gay thing, but I was becoming more open. And so at forty-five, finding my own way, I took another step closer to knowing who I was. Much of my sadness had lifted, but still I wasn't sure I'd ever be strong enough to face the challenges of my son's sexuality, in a less than tolerant world.

CHAPTER 5

COMING OUT

Life is not the way it's supposed to be. It's the way it is.
The way you cope with it is what makes the difference.
(Virginia Satir)

༄

The idea that parents of gay sons and daughters go through their own coming-out process was something I had never even given a thought to—until I became one of those parents. Then I spent a lot of time thinking about it, and came to see that the coming-out process was not exclusive to gay children. Parents come out too, and it's usually after a period of hibernation—how long the hibernation lasts and what awakens each of us is as individual as we are. That waking was for me pretty much a process of baby steps, until I joined the Foundation for Mideast Communication and took a giant leap forward.

Just a few months after I joined FMC, during meetings there was a lot of talk about the upcoming national convention in Los Angeles. A group from the Orlando Board was going to L.A. and even though I had no idea what to expect, I decided to go too. I was filled with excitement, along with a little fear. Syd was by this time reeling from all the changes in me. I was spreading my wings and knew this transformation wasn't easy for him. He never mentioned it, but there were times I thought he must be wondering, "What happened to the girl I married?" It was still me—but I was on a new road, going full speed ahead, discovering myself and new ways to be in the world. Although Syd hadn't caught up with me yet, he remained loving and supportive as always.

When my fellow Orlando Board members and I arrived at our hotel in Los Angeles, it was bustling with Arabs and Jews who had come together from all over the country for what was sure to be an interesting, experiential, and much different weekend than I ever experienced. During each day there was a variety of workshops, meetings, and discussion groups; evenings were spent getting to know each other. There was no shortage of conflict—never my strong suit, but even when exchanges got heated, what impressed me was that it was with a genuine spirit of bridge building. We were, after all, all children of Abraham, surprisingly more alike than we were different, and there was no denying the connection we shared. The weekend was eye opening. I found myself awakening to a world I never even knew existed with people who were open to the possibility of change, and were trying to make a difference in the world.

One of the main tenets of FMC was generous listening. This meant that instead of waiting for a chance to interrupt with a comeback, or thinking up arguments to drive home our point of view, we were to listen attentively to what was being said. This is easier said than done, especially with conversations as passionate as some of ours were. Listening generously, I discovered, was not the way most of us listened, and certainly not the way I did. So, that weekend I worked at putting my glaringly present reactivity in check and listening with my full attention. I did pretty well—a lot of the time, except when I didn't. It's not easy to pay attention at that level. It took a real shift in consciousness to focus, not so much on the words being said, but on the meaning and intention of what was left unsaid. Years later when I became a therapist, I found it good training.

One night after dinner a group of us were kibitzing, telling Arab and Jewish jokes, one after the other. It was a wonderful evening; the jokes were great fun and the laughter nonstop. But then the jokes became gay jokes, and suddenly, it was like someone switched the movie, and I was sitting in the middle of a horror film. I sat with a frozen smile on my face, until I couldn't stand it anymore, feigned jet lag, and said goodnight. Back in the safety of my room, I took a long hot shower, sobbing as I let the warm water run over me. An hour earlier, it had felt like my life had taken a whole new turn for the better, but when the gay jokes started, it brought me back short. "Will I ever get over this?" I wondered. I toweled off, put on a robe, and sat on the bed trying to pull myself together, when I heard Louise's key in the door.

We had met years earlier, in 1982, when I was part of the oral history program for the Holocaust Memorial Resource and Education Center of Central Florida. I had volunteered to interview survivors and liberators of the concentration camps. Louise was the director of the program. The interviews were being videotaped for the Holocaust Center's archives. The stories I heard from the three people I interviewed were profound; a liberator of the camps, a survivor, and a member of the resistance. It was an amazing program, and a tremendous learning experience, something I'm very proud to have been a part of. Now, six years later, Louise and I had become good friends and were sharing a room for the weekend. When she walked into the room my face was flushed from crying, and my eyes were red and swollen.

"Are you okay?" She asked.

"No," I told her, "I'm not."

"What's wrong?"

"I had to leave because of the gay jokes," I said... and then the floodgates opened. Between sobs I told Louise about Michael and oh, what a telling that was, as my pain and grief poured out into countless tissues. Louise listened with loving acceptance and empathy, and I felt a great unburdening. Since that night, she has been an ally, supporting me like a sister through the ups and downs of my coming out. The closeness we shared in Los Angeles grew into a deep friendship, and we continue to share each other's lives, crying, laughing, and celebrating together through whatever life sends our way. After that weekend I knew I was where I needed to be and I was ready for what would be the next step in my growth when Louise and Hedy began a Re-evaluation Counseling (RC) group for members of the Orlando Board of FMC.

Re-evaluation Counseling was new for me, but the theory made sense. The basic nature of human beings is to be loving, smart, trusting, creative, connected, and zestful. But in the course of our lives, some experiences caused us to close up and disconnect from our inherent nature, keeping us stuck in reactive behavior. Most of us know the feeling of having our "buttons pushed," being re-stimulated with old feelings of not being good enough, smart enough, attractive enough, thin enough, and so forth. An RC session works by having two people co-counsel one another, with one person acting as the counselor, while the other person acts as the client. Sessions are confidential. The client uses the time to discharge feelings, while the counselor listens, only offering help to increase the discharging. Then they switch roles. The theory is that by being heard in the presence of another person's loving attention, we can reclaim those shutdown parts of ourselves.

While doing RC, I woke one morning remembering a vivid dream I had about being locked out of my house. What I didn't realize until writing this is how similar the dream was to a real-life experience I actually had when I was nine years old (more about that later). In the dream I was locked out of my house, it was late, the lights were out and I was alone. As hard as I tried I couldn't seem to open the door; none of the keys fit. As I analyzed the dream, it seemed paradoxical, since by staying so closeted I was, in a very real sense, locked inside my house rather than out of it. But the more I thought about the dream; the irony was that what I was locked out of was not my house, but my life. It was time to unlock the door.

One of the people I met through FMC was Adele. A Christian, Arab, and former nun, Adele seemed at first an unlikely friend, but I was drawn to her spirituality and acceptance of people from all backgrounds. Often we had long philosophical talks, and found that we had more in common than not. Adele and I were co-counseling together in RC, and I called her to arrange a session. I honestly didn't know how she felt about gays but hoped she would be accepting and understanding.

During my session, I said, "Adele, there's something I have to tell you that's so hard for me...but here goes..." when I had finished, I waited anxiously for her reaction. Adele could see my nervousness and later said she couldn't imagine what I was going to say.

"I see how painful this is for you," she said. "Know that it's not an issue for me, and any way I can support you, I will. It's painful for me as well, to see how persecuted gays are, especially by the Church."

Relief flooded over me.

Shortly after that, Syd and I saw a segment on *60 Minutes* about Mel White. He had been an evangelical minister and had spent thirty-five years undergoing useless treatments from "ex-gay therapies" to exorcism, to electro-shock therapy, struggling to "overcome his sexual orientation." Before he came out, White worked as a speechwriter for Jerry Falwell, Jim Bakker, and Pat Robertson, all of whom were known for their disapproval of homosexuality. White was the ghostwriter for several of their books, including, Falwell's autobiography, *Strength for the Journey*. Of course Falwell and the others had no idea White was gay when he was working for them; White was married and closeted at the time. But when they found out, they immediately cut all ties to him. Now, ironically, White was way out and talking on national TV about his experiences with these high-profile evangelists.

I reported back to Adele how touched Syd and I were by his story. It turned out that she had read White's book, *Stranger at the Gate*, recounting the struggle he had accepting his sexual orientation. She gave us a copy of it.

White is now head of Soulforce, an organization working toward acceptance and freedom from religious and political oppression for gays and lesbians. Adele also introduced me to the wonderful writings of the brilliant and progressive Bishop John Shelby Spong, who makes the world a better place with his honesty and tolerance of all things, including homosexuality. Telling Adele had been easier than telling Louise, and so it was with each successive person.

Next came Rick. We had become fast friends and had been co-counseling together for several months. Fun and easy to be with, Rick had great depth and a loving heart, and from our first meeting, I felt like I had known him all my life. Rick and I fell into a routine of co-counseling together; it was comfortable and safe and over several months I worked through many issues—everything but Michael being gay. Then, during one session, I began processing how difficult it was for me to accept having a gay son. It wasn't something I planned to do, and I surprised myself by being so open about it. Rick, by listening with such wonderful attention and empathy, created a safe place for me to be real. For the next year we had many sessions together, where I felt the freedom to let go of that most unholy trinity of emotions: shame, blame, and guilt. During a friendship that began over twenty years ago, we've seen each other at our best and at our worst. In spite of that, or maybe because of it, our relationship has deepened and grown. With Rick I've always felt appreciated and accepted—for who I am. He doesn't pull any punches and I can count on him—Dr Rick, I call him. He's like the brother I always wished for. He and his wife Elizabeth are two of my most cherished friends.

About ten years ago, Syd, Rick and I started writing together. We began a partnership, TriBumpkin we called it; it seemed to us a fitting name. First we wrote a sitcom for TV, and then a romantic comedy script for the movies. They were damned good, and what fun we had! But, that's a whole other story.

Some of my friends from FMC had attended a growth course called UYO™ (Understanding Yourself and Others—pronounced U.Y.O.), developed by Global Relationship Centers, Inc.[3] They credited the course with helping them change their lives. And because I felt this almost indefinable force compelling me to shed the ill-fitting skin I'd worn for so much of my life, I signed up to take the course, scary as it was. It was a skin that no longer fit, and I was so ready to take it off, though wriggling out of it would be no easy job. UYO would be one of the most intense and challenging of the growth courses I took.

---

[3] Now called P3 (Personal Power and Prosperity)

But like a salmon making its way upstream, I was struggling to find my way home and so I kept moving forward.

After I signed up to take the course, Syd and I left on vacation to celebrate our twenty-fifth anniversary. The trip was charmed from beginning to end. When we got to the airport we were bumped up to business class, and when the inexpensive car we ordered wasn't available, we were given a high-end Mercedes. Was the universe supporting my decision? I thought so. I felt happy and relaxed until reality set in: I actually had to *go* to UYO! Then I was a complete wreck about it—who knew what I would have to face there? I was sure it would be my shame and fear about having a gay son. I didn't know if I was ready to deal with all of that—it was only about two years after Michael came out and except for a few friends who knew about it, I was still closeted. I wondered what I was letting myself in for. I'll never forget getting ready for the weekend. I was taking a shower and shaking so with fear, I could barely hold onto the soap.

But what I came face to face with that weekend wasn't anything about Michael, unexpectedly; it was about my mother, who was living near us in Orlando at the time. I was her only caregiver. The older she got, the more demanding and self-centered she got, and I felt a great deal of anger toward her and her unreasonable demands on me.

During one of many UYO sessions, I had the opportunity to do a role-play with a woman resembling my mother; I was trying to say no to her, but it wasn't going well. Each time I said no and walked away, the woman playing my mother would plead with me to come back; I kept going back. It was true that she needed me; that I was all she had. But, then "my mother" stopped begging and brought out the big guns. She demanded that I come back, telling me I owed her that, after all she had done for me. A good daughter would never leave her mother. *She* had never left *her* mother. There it was—the guilt my real mother knew how to use so expertly. That's when I felt my anger rising. The truth was that no matter how much I did for my mother, it was never enough; she always wanted more from me. How empowering it was to begin working through those issues, and to see just how much my mother's manipulation was affecting me.

At the end of the weekend I left a pile of emotional baggage behind, and felt a whole lot lighter. I went back to UYO many times and worked on many different issues. Each time I went it was always intense, but oh, how I grew. The first time was the hardest, each time after, it got easier.

I loved the sense of freedom I found there and wanted to share that with Syd, but no matter how I tried to convince him, I couldn't get him to go. Whenever I asked he'd say, "Isn't that the place you have to get up and howl like a dog?" It was, and we both knew it. Neither Syd nor Howard wanted any part of it, but about a year later Michael went to UYO, and then a few years after that Howard did too. They each went alone so they could have the safety they needed to work on their core issues. The course was as empowering for them as it was for me. But still

Syd wouldn't budge, so finally I gave up and stopped asking.

But a few years later, with Howard's encouragement, Syd finally bit the bullet, and he and I went to the course together. What an amazing weekend for us! We were all beginning to let go of unhealthy baggage, and were excited by what we were learning and how we were growing. The work we did during that time would bring us closer as a family, and help us to be so much more authentic with each other.

Soon I began to realize that some of the issues I was dealing with went very deep, and that what I was seeing was only a small piece of a very large iceberg. Over the years I would continue chipping away at it, one piece at a time. Meditation helped though it took a while to get the hang of it. The first time I tried it I turned the phone off, found a comfortable place to sit, took a few deep breaths, and I was meditating—but not for long. My mind was like a runaway train that wouldn't stop, and I thought, I could never do this. But the next day I tried again. This time I set a timer with the goal of meditating for one minute. It was one of the longest minutes of my life, but I stuck with it. Every day I made time to sit and meditate; before long, I was meditating for about twenty minutes a day. I became much more peaceful and centered. Stilling those internal voices rattling around in my head, even for a little while, was like taking a mini-vacation. One day during my meditation practice the wounded child in me, so in need of healing, showed up and I found myself crying unshed tears for all that I had lost when my father died. I had been carrying a heavy weight of sadness about his death for years. During meditation, I was able to grieve that loss. I also cried for the ways I had been abandoned by others, and for all the ways I had abandoned myself. Often there were times I didn't know what the tears were about, but when a wave of sadness enveloped me, I didn't try to understand; I just allowed myself to feel it. There are some things that can't be understood with the head, they can only be felt from the heart.

When I was growing up, learning was never easy for me, and I was less than a stellar student, just squeaking by in school. No one knew about learning disorders back then, which was too bad, because I had one that I didn't discover until I went back to college. When I had trouble understanding a concept, particularly in math, my mother, a first-class bookkeeper, proficient in math, would try to explain it to me, but would quickly lose patience.

"It's so simple," she would say, exasperated when I didn't get it—simple for her maybe, but not for me. Hearing that I wasn't very smart enough times, I came to believe it, and like many children in a similar situation, I was smart enough to figure out that I wasn't smart enough. Rather than suffer my mother's displeasure, I struggled through school the best I could.

A story my mother loved to tell was of my second-grade teacher, Mrs. Schroeder, saying, "Enid will never set the world on fire scholastically, but she'll do fine out in the world. She gets along well with the other children." That was very important to my mother, more so than good grades. I was, she believed, only a girl, and just needed to be smart enough to get a good husband.

Every time I heard that story, it affirmed how inadequate I felt when it came to my ability to learn. I carried those feelings around with my schoolbooks, from grade school, through college, and into my marriage with Syd. In RC, I spent many sessions working on my hurt and distress around feeling not smart enough, until I was finally able to reclaim my inherent intelligence.

With Syd's encouragement, in the late 1980's I decided to go back to school part time. Each semester I took a few classes; my first semester it was humanities, creative writing, and English literature. For the first time I loved being in school. I even enjoyed doing the homework (most of the time) and looked forward to my classes. College was a whole new experience. It was like a window shade in my head was being lifted and I could see so much more of the world. Michael and Howard were teenagers then, and each night at the dinner table we had lively discussions about what we learned that day. It was a fun, exciting time for me.

When I was graduating from college in 1992 I was asked to join Phi Kappa Phi National Honor Society. It was quite a kick for me, and I called Syd right away and proudly told him. That night my precious husband came home with a dozen red roses with a card saying, "Congratulations Honey, for setting the world on fire scholastically." I laughed when I first read the card, then, I cried, realizing I actually had set the world on fire scholastically. Mrs. Schroeder had made a mistake. How I wished I could have found her and told her!

What a corrective experience that was for me. A few weeks later, in May of that year, I became the last person in our family to graduate from college. Syd had come first, years earlier, then Michael, and then Howard, whose graduation was just two days before mine. We had quite a celebration.

I took the summer off and started graduate school in the fall. The summer wasn't the only thing I took off. The "not smart enough label" that I had carried around since childhood was finally gone; I let it go.

In grad school one of my favorite classes was group counseling. There were twenty-seven of us in the class and by the end of the semester we had become an intimate, cohesive group. The last night of the class, my professor, Dr. Rini, asked us to put our name at the top of a blank sheet of paper and pass our paper to the person on our right. Each person then anonymously wrote a comment, and passed the paper to their right until everyone had written something about each person in the class.

When I got my paper back, I glanced over it and focused on the comment, "cold and distant." Hmm, I got stuck on that one. I couldn't imagine who would describe me that way. When we were processing this exercise, I asked who wrote it. A young woman raised her hand. Dr. Rini skillfully worked through her feelings, and then asked me what I learned from the exercise.

"What I learned was that there were twenty-six people throwing beautiful bouquets at me, filled with words like balanced, loving, nurturing, encouraging...one person threw a ball of crap—and that's the one I caught."

Everyone laughed. It was funny and broke the tension, but it was so true—not just for me but for others in the class. I made it a goal to remember to choose the bouquets and duck when those balls started coming.

The small circle of people we met through FMC was continuing to grow. Soon Syd and I were meeting an eclectic group of intelligent, genuine, well-read, and open-minded people. My world was opening up and it didn't take long before one by one, I began letting them know that I had a gay son: Lynn was first, next came Linda, then Dawn and Maria, and later Elizabeth. Each was empathically supportive and continues to be so.

One night at an FMC meeting Louise told us about a rabbi, one of the fathers of Jewish Renewal, Reb Zalman Schachter-Shalomi, who would be in South Florida for a Shabbaton weekend later that month. None of us had ever heard of him or knew what a Shabbaton weekend was. (a spiritual celebration of the Sabbath from Friday night through Saturday night).

"From everything I've read, he's exceptional, not to be missed. We have to go," Louise insisted. When some of us expressed doubt, Louise said, "Trust me. You won't be sorry." We weren't.

Taking Louise at her word, twelve of us, including Syd, went together for what turned out to be an extraordinary weekend, spent chanting, singing, dancing, laughing and crying together. There were all kinds of people there from all branches of Judaism. One woman I met identified as a JewBu (Jewish Buddhist). I had never heard of that before. She said that practicing Buddhist meditation along with Judaism brought her greater clarity and had deepened her spiritual connection to Judaism. She, like me and many others were there looking for something that would feed our spiritual souls. What opened my heart was seeing openly gay people there who were fully accepted and treated like anyone else, and it gave me hope. It was another step forward.

From my experience the three main branches of Judaism (Orthodox, Conservative, and even Reform—this was over twenty years ago), shunned gays, and if my religion shunned my son because he was gay, then they also shunned me. Feeling alienated, I began to distance myself from my religion; it had been a long time coming. After my father's death, when Michael was just eighteen months old, I gradually began letting go of some of the rituals I had practiced all my life and became less religiously observant. The biggest change was when I stopped keeping kosher. It was a declaration of sorts that I was angry with God for taking my father from me. I still attended synagogue with Syd and the kids, and we celebrated Jewish holidays, but I didn't feel a spiritual connection. I was just going through the motions. But that Friday night, I found myself awakening to the spirituality I had so hungered for, and when I prayed to God, it was the first time I could remember feeling that God was listening. In Jewish Renewal, the spark of Judaism, so different from what I saw as the ossified religion of my child-hood, was rekindled in me. Reb Zalman did more than bring a congregation of seekers together into a spiritually connected community. That weekend, he led me and many others back to our core.

It was now six years since Michael dropped his bombshell on us, and I was becoming more open; the fear of anyone "knowing" had lost some of its charge. I felt better about myself and with the people around me, and I made a choice not to have anyone in my life, from that point on, with whom I couldn't be real. I had done enough pretending and keeping secrets. Finally I was coping with having a gay son and coming out, if not to my family of origin, at least to the family of choice that I was creating.

CHAPTER 6

ALL IN THE FAMILY

*If you have a tail of straw, it's best not to get too
close to the fire.*
(Anonymous)

᠙

Coming out to families can be tricky, and Syd's
and mine were no exception. What got in our way
was not so much the fear of how our families would
react, although I don't want to minimize that. It was
huge for us, but that wasn't the underlying issue.
Over time, as in every family, Syd and I had been
on the receiving end of hurtful experiences and comments from family members that we didn't know
how to deal with. So, in the name of keeping peace,
we swept them under the proverbial rug where such
things get swept.

Everything remained at status quo until Michael
came out, then it seemed like all that stuff we had
shoved so conveniently under the rug came seeping
out all over the place. We weren't sure what to do
with it but knew it needed cleaning up.

About four years after "coming out day," Michael
said he wanted to tell the rest of the family about his

sexual orientation. We told him we weren't ready. Of course we knew at some point they would have to know. But while we had come a far way, we hadn't come that far—not yet.

Hedy once asked me why we felt the need to protect our families. I told her we weren't protecting *them*; we were protecting *us*. Syd and I knew that telling them would be akin to diving headlong into a wasp's nest, which would have been easier for us to do and a whole lot less painful.

We could predict our families' reactions. There would be a million questions to try to get to the bottom of things, which in itself would be enough of a nightmare. But in the end someone would have to be blamed. Syd and I had just spent the last few years navigating through the most turbulent seas; now we felt the need to stay on dry land, for a while anyway, before jumping back into that stormy water. Until we worked through some of the layers of our unfinished business, if not with family members directly, at least within ourselves, telling them would have to wait.

I couldn't even imagine what would ensue if my mother knew. There was no way she could come to terms with having a gay grandson. She would see Michael as a negative reflection of herself and too much of a *shunda* for her ever to accept. The bottom line was, my mother didn't want to know what she didn't want to know, and that she had a gay grandson definitely fit into that category. As I write this, it's been nineteen years since her death, and not telling her is something I've never regretted. For all of my life my mother's essential concern was what other people thought of her, her children, and later her grandchildren. Looking different, or appearing wrong in any way, was something she could not bear. Appearances were everything.

Here's a revealing example that shows what I mean. When I was seven years old our dentist, Dr. Sokoloff, was drafted into the army. My uncle suggested we go to a golfing buddy of his, Dr. Laskey, whose office was nearby. As soon as I walked into the office, I had an uneasy feeling. The waiting room, filled with old, shabby furniture, had a dank, musty smell, and beneath a bay window were some scrawny plants. We sat down and in a few minutes an assistant ushered me into Dr. Laskey's office. Laskey breezed in, all business; there was no small talk. He looked in my mouth without so much as a hello.

"You have a cavity," He announced, taking out his drill.

"Dr. Sokoloff always gave me Novocaine," I said, in a small, uncertain voice.

"It's a small cavity," he said, "You won't even feel it."

I wasn't too sure about that, but figured, he's the dentist so he must know what he's doing. When he began drilling, I felt a twinge of pain and held up my hand, the way Dr. Sokoloff taught me to do, expecting him to stop. But he didn't, so I moved his arm. Whoa...he didn't like that—one bit. He pulled my arm away, telling me to sit still and stop being a baby; he'd be done in a minute. When he started drilling, again I felt pain, grabbed his arm, and this time yanked it away.

Furious, Laskey began shouting at me. In rushed my mother–to my rescue? Hardly. Her concern was not that some callous dentist was causing her daughter pain; she was embarrassed by my outburst. When, to appease the doctor, she told me to sit still and behave, I jumped out of the chair, yanked the dental cloth from my neck, and tearfully ran out of the office.

Later, mortified by my actions, my mother chastised me. What would Dr. Laskey think of me? Think of her? Think of our family? What would my uncle say? According to my mother, I was a willful, spoiled brat (what she called me whenever I did something she didn't like). Was I to sit and be abused quietly? I suppose so.

Terrified by the experience, I didn't go back to a dentist until I was fifteen years old, with a wisdom tooth that needed pulling and a mouthful of cavities.

Here's what I learned: The feelings of an inconsequential stranger, who my mother would never see again, were more important to her than I was. That I was being hurt and mistreated was of no consequence. What mattered to my mother was I had gone against her 11th Commandment: Never, ever, do anything to embarrass your mother. And of course I had done just that; I made her look bad, and she lost face.

To this day I marvel that I found the courage to get out of there. If under those circumstances my mother was incapable of standing up for her own daughter, would she now rise to the occasion and accept having a gay grandson? There was no way that would happen. As much as I needed support and a safe haven, I knew I'd get neither from my mother. She simply wasn't emotionally available.

As a child and a young adult, whenever I needed help or advice, or someone to talk to, it had been my father I went to. He had always listened and understood me like no one else, but would he have understood this? And would I have had the nerve to tell him? Probably not. Both he and my mother were from the old school, the one that said being gay was a *shunda*.

Then there was the fear of my father's horrific temper; it seemed to be attached to a very short fuse that could blow at any moment. I learned early on to read my father's moods. This may have been good training for when I became a therapist, but growing up his outbursts terrified me. This poem I wrote years ago captures my uncertainty when it came to my father's often unpredictable nature:

<u>Watching</u>

My father used to peel an apple
in one long continuous swirl.
I watched as the peel grew longer,
coiling and curling
like a ringlet of freshly permed hair.
All the while watchful
for signs
of change,
from calm
to anger
to rage.

> The changing seemed to come
> without warning
> like a summer storm.
> What if the peel broke?
> I worried and watched, fearing
> his mood would give way
> to anger
> ending the moment
> of tranquility.

Depending on his mood, my father could be patience personified, calm and easygoing one day, the next raging at the world. And I never knew what to expect. Anything could set him off. How well I recall the summer when I was eight years old. My father took my sister and me out for a ride in his new car. Whenever he got behind the wheel, the only thing we knew for sure was that it would be an interesting experience. So we were driving along, I don't remember where, telling jokes and having a fun time when suddenly my father sat up a bit straighter. That was my signal: hold onto your hat. In a instant he was off and running.

"Did you see that guy?" He'd ask. "That son of a bitch cut me off. Who the hell does he think he is? I'll show him."

My sister and I exchanged a knowing glance; we were in for a rough ride. It was road rage, before it had a name. But for all his *mishagas* (craziness) I adored my father and never had any doubt how much he loved me. He would have been the one person in my family I might have told.

When it came to Syd's family, the picture was equally bleak. We didn't doubt that Syd's father would remain loving to Michael, whom he adored. That wasn't the issue; the issue was his attitude toward Syd and me. Over the years, Syd's dad had become more and more shut down and bitter. A good deal of that bitterness was directed toward Syd, who kept his distance to avoid his father's cutting, sarcastic jabs. It seemed no matter what we did, my father-in-law knew a better way, a smarter way to do it. He seemed to take pleasure in finding fault with whatever we did—the way we lived, shopped, cooked, it even bothered him to see us hold hands. Tell him about Michael? I don't think so. That would have only given him more ammunition to criticize us.

Then, in the space of six weeks, the landscape changed dramatically. First Syd's father, and then my mother both died. We went from one funeral to the next with hardly enough time to catch our breath. Neither of our parents had been in the best of health, but we never expected either of them to go downhill so quickly. Their deaths so close together, and so unexpected threw our lives into chaos. I remember at my mother's funeral having the realization that I had moved to the top rung of my family hierarchy. There were no parents or grandparents, no aunts or uncles there to shelter me; I had become the matriarch. It left me with an uneasy feeling. Both Syd's family and mine had been part of each other's lives for over thirty years; now, burying two of our parents was not only difficult for us, but for other family members as well. It seemed the problem we were having, of how and when to come out, at least with Syd's father and my mother had unfortunately taken care of itself.

When it came to telling his mother about Michael, Syd and I weren't ready for that to happen. Our concern wasn't that her feelings toward Michael would change; it was how she might react toward us. While she was fiercely loyal to her family, she was also hypercritical and could be incredibly harsh.

For so many years of our relationship, I had found it difficult, if not impossible, to please her. But being a pleaser, God knows, I tried. She was one tough cookie—harsh, opinionated, headstrong, and domineering. I used to imagine making a tape recording of her when she was on a rant, so she could hear just how harsh she sounded. No one, except for Syd's dad, ever had the nerve to confront her about it.

In the early years of my marriage how I dreaded when my mother-in-law came for a visit. She would go through every room in our apartment, opening closets, cabinets, and drawers, inspecting everything. Back then I didn't know enough to say, "excuse me, but this is my house, not yours, and I'm fine with things the way they are." I had no boundaries then and neither did she. So I stood silently by as she proceeded to hurl insults at me while emptying my cabinets and rearranging everything in them to her liking.

"Who lives like this?" She would say, as she examined my pantry closet. Not waiting for my answer to her rhetorical question, she would respond, "Pigs live like this. Is it so hard to keep things orderly? It takes five minutes."

When she was finished straightening the pantry it was on to the linen closet. "What kind of a mother doesn't teach her daughter how to fold towels?" she would say with disgust as she re-folded my towels and neatly lined them up in the closet. Evidently mine. The correct way to fold towels, I learned, was the way my mother-in-law did it. Granted, when it came to housekeeping, I was not in her league. Anyone could open her cabinets, drawers, and closets at any time of the day or night and find them in perfect order. If there had been a category in the Olympics for neatness, my mother-in-law would have brought home the gold.

How different our relationship might have been if she had asked if I wanted her help and did so without the critical comments. I would have welcomed it. The good news was that when she left, my cabinets were in order; the bad news was my emotional state was in disarray. Through the years I learned to stay away to avoid my mother-in-law's unexpected and often unexplained outbursts.

I wasn't about to open myself up to her critical scrutinizing and questioning about Michael, nor was Syd—not with her so immersed in her grief. And with all of our emotions so raw; it didn't feel like the right time to open that door.

Even though my encounters with my mother-in-law were often troubled and problematic, she was the most loving grandmother and had a wonderful relationship with both Michael and Howard. She may have found it difficult to show affection to her children, but such was not the case when it came to her grandchildren.

Now, after fifty-two years of marriage, Syd's mother was struggling to adjust to being on her own after the loss of her husband. Michael was in medical school at the time, and living not far from her, so he moved in with her for a few months to keep her company and help in whatever way he could. Naturally he wanted to tell his grandmother about his sexual orientation then; they had always been close, never more than during this period, and Michael knew that nothing would change that. When Syd and I explained to Michael that our relationship with Syd's mother was much different than his, he respected our need to work through our own issues before coming out to her.

The idea of telling my sister was daunting too. We were worlds apart from one another, geographically and emotionally, and our relationship was strained at best. Absorbed in her life, my sister was unaware of and indifferent to what was going on in mine. Based on our past relationship, she wasn't someone I would have expected to be supportive or understanding. And, again, Michael was willing to let us take our time with her.

The only person Michael pressured us to come out to was Syd's sister. They had a close relationship and her not knowing was becoming uncomfortable for him since she was constantly trying to fix him up with women.

"It's ruining our relationship," he told us. "The first ten minutes of every conversation is about who I'm dating or who she wants to fix me up with."

But Syd and I weren't ready to open that door either. Still, Michael kept pushing and one day asked, "Dad, have you told another living soul that I'm gay?"

"No, " Syd said. "I'm okay with it. Why, should I?"

"Don't you think you should look at that, Dad?" Michael asked.

Syd was struck by Michael's words. Until then he hadn't realized that, by being in the closet, he was limiting Michael. But after that conversation, he did. A short while later he told Michael he needed three months, and after that he would be okay with his sister knowing. Why three months? I don't know, but somehow giving himself a finite period of time seemed to open a door for Syd.

I was reluctant to tell Syd's sister. There was no doubt in my mind that she would be there for Syd, simply because he was the brother she adored, but I wasn't at all sure she would be supportive of me. At that time she believed the old myth that men became gay because of something their mother did. When Michael did come out to her, she told him she had always known, and it made no difference at all to her. She loved him and nothing he could ever do or say would change that; she would always be there for him.

Telling families—not fun—not even close, whether it's our children telling us, or us telling family members. They are usually the last ones to know, since the coming out process is not a linear one. In reality it's much more circular, as it was for me and is for most people, I've learned. In my case first I told a small circle of friends about Michael, then I expanded the circle to the next level, one person at a time. As I felt safe enough, I went to the level after that in ever broadening circles. What kept us from coming out to our families was more about our dysfunctional relationships with them than it was about Michael being gay. Not surprisingly, it is for many families.

CHAPTER 7

THE JEWISH CONNECTION

*A man
can't make a place
for himself in the sun,
if he keeps taking refuge
under the family tree.*
(Helen Keller)

∽

When I was growing up I lived within a few blocks of my mother's large, close-knit family. They were so close-knit that coming home from school, if I sneezed on the corner, by the time I walked to the end of the block, the whole family knew it. Both of my parents' families had fled Russia to escape years of shtetles, persecution, and pogroms. Along with whatever belongings they could carry with them, they also had in tow their deep fear and distrust of gentiles. They came to America in search of the land of opportunity, the Golden Medina, where the streets, they were told, were paved with gold. What they found was far more precious than the metal they had been promised: religious freedom and tolerance to practice their beliefs without fear of reprisals.

My mother was the last child of seven brothers and sisters; the only one of her siblings born in the United States after her parents emigrated from Russia in the early 1900s. When I look back to my early childhood, it seems like everyone I came in contact with, with only a few exceptions was Jewish. My mother had a deep distrust of gentiles and did her best to keep them as far away as possible. With time, she became less fearful, but for much of her life, she painstakingly distanced herself from anyone too far outside the boundary of our narrow family circle. After her death, while we were sitting *Shiva* (the Jewish mourning period), a childhood friend came to pay a condolence call.

"Do you remember when we were kids," Peggy said. "How your mother wouldn't let us play together until she was sure that I was Jewish?"

"I do," I said. "I remember it well, and you weren't the only one of my friends who was cross-examined."

After my family moved from our very Jewish neighborhood in West Philadelphia to the more assimilated Overbrook Hills, only those kids who were Jewish got my mother's stamp of approval. The funny thing was, I always had gentile friends in school, but that didn't seem to cause my mother much concern. I'm not really sure why, but I suppose at school it was out of sight, out of mind.

Although he had his share of prejudice, my father was more open-minded than my mother, and his best friend was Irish Catholic. When our family was invited to their home for Sunday dinner, my mother wasn't comfortable about going, so my father took me. They were a warm, loving bunch, and I didn't know why my mother made such a big deal about it. But when dinner was served it didn't take long to figure it out; the main course was ham. I remember looking at the large ham sitting in the middle of the table with curious fascination. Coming from a kosher home, it was the first time I had ever seen a ham, and it didn't look or smell like anything I had ever seen before. Had she been there that night, my Orthodox mother would have been so offended she would likely have excused herself from the table, and left posthaste.

I couldn't fathom why my father's good friends would insult us this way. Didn't they know we were kosher and that our Jewish dietary laws prohibited us from eating pork? It didn't make sense. Then it dawned on me: they didn't know—my father hadn't told them. Was he afraid of being seen as too different in his friend's eyes? That's what I concluded. I didn't want to embarrass my father or his friend, so I never said a word and ate around the ham, which I carefully hid under a mound of mashed potatoes.

Later, when my mother heard about the evening, it affirmed her reason for not going, and reinforced her belief that to be safe, it was best not to venture too far from her own self-contained world.

As it does for all of us, my parents' history became the template for who and what was safe in their world. Gentiles, with rare exceptions, were not safe, and over time became a category, symbolizing anyone too different from us. Like the "Others," the fictional characters on the TV program *Lost*, most of my family believed Gentiles meant us harm, and were not to be trusted.

My family and so many other Jewish people felt the need to excel in whatever we did and *never*, (God forbid) do anything that would bring shame on ourselves, or on our families. It was a widely held belief, if we did do something considered shameful by others that would add to the considerable anti-Semitism already in the universe, which would then make the world a less safe place for the Jewish people. (With the shocking Bernie Madoff investment scandal that erupted in late 2008, that fear has been revived). Most Jewish people, especially those from my generation, have felt that we had to be better, and do better than others, simply to stay on an even keel—a tall order—grande actually.

So what was it about my religion that made homosexuality such a *shunda?* Culturally, nothing is more important to Jewish people than the family, and the passing down of our traditions. There are built-in expectations that our sons and daughters will marry, have children, and carry forth our traditions, from one generation to another. Homosexuality precluded that, so there was no place for gays, and no acceptance. They were seen as second-class citizens, choosing to live on the fringe of society, disrespecting all that the Jewish people held dear, and therefore deserving of our contempt. It's taken a long time to begin changing those beliefs and attitudes about homosexuality. There has been progress in the Conservative, and certainly Reform movements that reflect a new understanding of human sexuality. Not so in Jewish Orthodoxy.

Now, as I think about it, the information I received to categorize gays was unmistakably homophobic, but it flew above the radar. When the subject came up, it was usually with a contemptuous look, posture, or sneer, and of course there would be the word *fagele*, said condescendingly in a withering whisper. There was no doubt that gays were disregarded, discounted, and disrespected by pretty much everyone around me. That was the unchallenged norm and not up for discussion. Not that those beliefs were exclusive to the people who traveled in my circles. Prejudice toward gays was widely accepted throughout the gentile community, as well as in the Jewish community. That's just the way it was and I never gave it much thought; not many people I knew did.

Until shortly after my marriage I pretty much practiced my parents' Judaism. Conservadox, I called it, kind of a cross between Conservative and Orthodox, though leaning more toward the Conservative side. But that changed when I was twenty-two and my father became critically ill. Suddenly my world was turned upside down.

Daddy was the person in my family I was closest to; I adored him. Growing up how I loved waking up Saturday mornings and climbing into bed with him; we'd cuddle up and I'd listen to stories of his outrageous adventures. He left his abusive home at sixteen and traveled around the country doing whatever work he could find to support himself. He worked as a singing disc jockey, a cowboy, and even played baseball in the minor leagues as a shortstop and catcher. He would have made that his career, but his nose was broken so many times he had to quit. When something needed fixing in our house we never called a repairman, we called daddy. He could fix anything from televisions, to washing machines, to cars.

I always loved my father's spirit of adventure. One summer when I was five and a half, my father took my mother, sister and me on a trip around the country. He wanted his girls to see something more of the world than what was in our own backyards. Our old car broke down regularly, but my father would fix it and we traveled on, all around the country. If we had a radio in the car I don't remember, but I do remember my father serenading us, even yodeling sometimes when the mood struck him. He had a beautiful voice and a special love for what he called cowboy songs. We had a Coleman stove that he'd cook on and there were times we slept in some pretty dreadful places. Saying we roughed it would be quite an understatement. My mother and sister spent much of the trip in the back seat complaining of carsickness. But my father and I paid them little mind; we were having too much fun.

He was my rock. He never got sick, not even a cold, so it was a terrible shock when my mother told me that the exhaustion he had been experiencing was much more serious than we had ever imagined. He had acute leukemia and there was nothing anyone could do to help him. I felt completely powerless as I watched my father wasting away before my eyes. Only months later he died at age fifty-two. I was profoundly affected by his death, and now, even more than forty years later, the depth of that loss is immeasurable. Angry at God for leaving me in a world without my father, piece by piece as the years went by, I began throwing away not only the husk of my religion, but the kernel as well.

Because it was important to him, I wanted to honor my father by saying *Kaddish*, (the Jewish prayer said daily for a period of twelve months after the death of a parent, spouse, child, or sibling, by those remaining). In Orthodox Judaism, customarily this prayer is said by men, not women. But, my father had no sons. So I went to a nearby Conservative synagogue each day to say *Kaddish*, but was not counted as part of the *Minyan* (ten men who gather to say prayers).

"Stay home and take care of your family," the men at the synagogue told me patronizingly. Eventually I stopped going. What was the point? I stayed home and said *Kaddish* for my father without the benefit of a *Minyan*. Not that it mattered; the fact was, according to Jewish law, as a woman, my voice did not count. It was a familiar feeling. When I was about five or six I remember being relegated upstairs to the balcony of our West Philadelphia synagogue, along with all the women who came for services. Only men were allowed downstairs, where the Torah was being read. Peeking my head out through the railing, I watched from the balcony, the men praying, feeling like an outsider at a party I hadn't been invited to.

As time went by, I began drifting further and further away from my religion and what I saw as a stifling straitjacket of rules. After seeing a billboard for a restaurant that announced, "No Rules, Just Right," I realized how Judaism had become the reverse for me: no rights, just rules. And I could no longer relate to the male-dominated religion I was brought up with. I had felt there was no place for me then, and years later, after Michael's coming out, no place for my family. I was spiritually hungry for something more. Where to find it? I didn't know. It wasn't until the Shabbaton weekend with Reb Zalman that I began reclaiming my spiritual connection to Judaism. Ironically, my understanding of where I stood in that Jewish world came when I joined the Foundation for Mideast Communication, and began to open to a world completely unfamiliar to me. It was a world of people with religions and cultures very different than my own. What I came to see was that the world was a much bigger place than I had ever imagined.

CHAPTER 8

ABOUT SHAME

The people we have contact with
are chisels and hammers who craft what we will become.
Our life's journey is an ever unfolding work of art
that tells the story of where we have been,
and with whom we have traveled.
(Iyanla Vanzant)

∾

It's not hard to notice that shame keeps weaving its way through the tapestry of my life, so I thought I'd explore a few of the whys and wherefores of it. Growing up there was always an undercurrent of anti-Semitism swirling about, and being Jewish, I felt I had to be cautious, in what sometimes was an unfriendly gentile world. So, like my family, I kept a low profile and tried to fit in and not call attention to myself. Anti-Semitism in the 1950s was nothing like what my grandparents and parents experienced; for one thing, it was much more subtle, but still, we all felt the sting of it. It's not like anyone was shooting at us with a loaded gun, but the message from the gentile community was clear; we were pretty low on the totem pole.

When I was in junior high school, most country clubs were restricted. How well I remember passing one on my way to school each day that had a sign posted on a perfectly manicured lawn saying, "No Jews or Dogs Allowed." No one seemed to think anything of it. If they did, no one was talking about it, except in the Jewish community. The dogs weren't barking any more or less. When the restriction was lifted at a few of Philadelphia's trendiest country clubs, two of my wealthy uncles became members at what they lovingly called "The Club." They couldn't have been happier if they owned the winning horse at the Kentucky Derby, which would have made them very happy indeed.

Now the sign on the lawn of the country club I passed each day, said only, "No Dogs Allowed," and things went on as before, but not much had changed. Jewish people were still the object of discrimination, even the rich ones who could afford to belong to a country club. The message was clear: gentiles may let us belong to their clubs, but accept us? We were still looked down on, treated as *less than*. And after being on the receiving end of that spoken and unspoken message long enough, pretty soon you begin to believe there's something wrong with you. Over time, that kind of shaming treatment will negatively color the perception of who you are. Incidents like this may in themselves, add only a cover of shame, but that covering can accumulate, and cling to you, like snow, resting on the branches of a tree.

After his untimely death in 2008, I heard a story about Tim Russert, moderator of "Meet the Press," that describes how feelings of being shamed can

linger for a lifetime. After a nun who was an important part of his life introduced him to journalism,
she helped him go to the more competitive Canisius
High School, a "better" school than the one he attended. But coming from humble beginnings, Russert had misgivings about what he described as, "A
fancy pants school on the other side of town."

At Canisius, Russert had to wear a tie as part of
the dress code. He did—it was a clip-on tie. He wore
it every day, until a history teacher tore the tie off
and, humiliating him in front of the class, "held it at
arm's length, like a dead skunk." Shamed, Russert
slunk home. When he told his father what happened,
his dad took him upstairs and taught his son how to
tie a Windsor knot. He wore a tie with that knot for
the rest of his life—he never wore a clip-on tie again.
Even though Russert went on to be a great journalist and newscaster, that shaming moment was one
that he remembered for the rest of his life.

The famous therapist Virginia Satir once said
that 96% of all families are dysfunctional. Which
brings us to another important cause of shame. Like
most families, mine was right up there with rest of
Satir's 96%. Loaded with guilt, denial, and shame
for starters, we were one extremely dysfunctional
bunch. Some of the unhealthy patterns we excelled at
were yelling, raging, isolating, verbal abuse, physi-
cal abuse, and let's not forget the silent treatment. It
was used so often in our house, we had a name for it:
"The Gaslight Treatment," after the movie, *Gaslight*,
with Ingrid Bergman, which, as I recall, was used to
drive Bergman's character crazy. Crazy-making or
not, all were sure-fire ways to create low self worth

and feelings of shame, whether that's what you're going for or not. One thing was certain: we weren't The Nelsons of *Ozzie and Harriet* fame, but then again neither were Ozzie and Harriet. They were just as dysfunctional as the rest of us, except when they were portraying a "perfect" family on their TV show.

My parents did the best they could, but being first generation Americans with a strong desire to fit in, and a need to prove themselves, they were caught in the middle of two worlds. With one foot in the old world of their parents (the Yiddish-speaking villages of Tsarist Russia), and the other foot in the new world of their children, they were carrying so much baggage, they often had a hard time keeping their lives balanced. For the most part, my parents were loving, intelligent, kind-hearted people, except when they were being judgmental, demanding, and perfectionistic. Interestingly, I found these same traits mirrored in most of the Jewish people I knew.

To survive my childhood, I developed defenses against being shamed, like perfectionism and people pleasing, which accompanied me into adulthood. I was very good at them. Later I would learn that no matter what I did, how pleasing I was, or even if I was the most perfect person on the planet, someone would manage to find fault with me anyway. Remember the old saying, "You can please some of the people some of the time, and most of the people..." well, you know the rest. Whoever said it, had that right. It would take many years before I became aware of my ingrained patterns and made the connection that pleasing others and making their needs more important than my own, was a sure way to lose myself.

Of course it wasn't their intention to instill in me a sense of insecurity and inadequacy, but because they lived such unconscious lives, that's just what my parents did. I think for my parents and a lot of other Jewish parents being good enough—wasn't enough—their offspring had to be *better than*, to make up for their shortcomings. It took the upheaval of Michael's coming out for me to begin peeling away the layers of my childhood experiences and gain an understanding of where my feelings came from. A story will illustrate:

When I was nine years old, my mother arranged for me to babysit for our neighbor's kids, who were not much younger than I. When the neighbors came home at midnight, they paid me 50 cents an hour—I was thrilled. When they didn't offer to take me home, I walked—by myself. It was a cold, moonless November night, so I hurried, taking a short cut through our neighbor's back yard. By the time I got home, I was frightened and out of breath. No light was on at our front door and I realized I didn't have a key to the house, so I knocked; no one answered. Afraid to ring the bell of my house, I went next door, where our cousins Sid and Louise lived, since they had a spare key. I kept ringing their bell until finally my cousin Sid sleepily answered.

When I told him what happened, he asked angrily, "What the hell are you waking me up for? Why don't you wake up your parents?"

Good question. I didn't have an answer. Peeved, Sid walked me home and as soon as he opened the door, embarrassed, I quickly said good night and went to my room.

The next day everyone listened to Sid's story of how I woke him up in the middle of the night, and they knocked themselves out making fun of me— for days. At the time, I didn't know why I woke Sid up instead of my parents. Now I do. Knowing my father's unpredictable temper, waking him was too scary a thought. And wake my mother? Waking her for any reason would be met with constant *kvetching* (complaining) that she couldn't get back to sleep or function the next day. That would be my fault. My grandmother, who lived with us, would likely have joined in too, wailing her favorite refrain, "What are you going to do with this child"…which would likely be followed by something like…"waking everyone up…she thinks of no one but herself." And my sister, given the opportunity to shift the family's attention from her to me, would be only too happy to join in.

What was most hurtful was being made to feel as though *I* was the one who had done something wrong. The reality was that no one in my family had thought to give me a key, make sure the door was left open, arrange to have someone bring me home, or even leave the light on. So what I learned from that experience, albeit unconsciously, was that I was expendable and my parents could simply forget about me. If I wanted to avoid being abandoned or mocked, I'd better tread ever so carefully, perfectly, doing whatever was expected of me. I didn't wake my parents that night because I was afraid to. At the age of nine, I knew it wasn't safe to ring the bell at my house, so I went where it was. This story may be unique to me, but we all have such stories, which, like a brush, paint on the landscape of who we are.

Unfortunately, I accepted the messages my parents covertly sent and internalized the shame and blame for how I was treated. Denying my parents' misdoing, I believed I was at fault. It's interesting how children can't bear to think of their parents as anything less than perfect. To keep that fantasy alive, children, even those fully-grown, will internalize their parents' unacceptable behavior and make themselves responsible, as I did. As though blaming them would somehow sever the invisible umbilical cord connecting us. It took many years before I understood that my personal history had been the source of many of the feelings, both negative and positive, that I had about myself. Out in the world I was to find those feelings affirmed over and over again, when others gave me messages that were similar to ones I had gotten from my family. Often, I found my reaction would be to blame myself, even without rationale.

My relationship with Syd's mother was another case in point. When Syd and I were dating, I learned the hard way that his mother was a screamer and that her behavior could be unpredictable. She and I started off on rocky footing when a friend and I thought it would be fun to take our boyfriends' little sisters out to dinner and to a movie. When we got to the theater and saw that the movie, three and a half hours long, wasn't going to be over until 11:30 p.m., I called Syd's house; his father answered. I explained the situation and asked if it was okay to stay out so late. It was summer, and he said not to worry, it would be fine. I promised to have my twelve-year old future sister-in-law home by midnight. As soon as the movie was over, we headed home. When we turned the corner toward Syd's house, there was his mother standing outside, pacing up and down in her bathrobe. I opened the car door, and the screaming began.

"What kind of person would keep a twelve-year-old child out until this hour of the night? Who would do such a thing? Where were you? I was ready to call the police."

Stunned by her outburst, I tried to explain that I had spoken to Mr. Jackowitz earlier and he had said it would be okay. But Syd's mother wasn't listening. She was too furious. Unfortunately, Syd's dad fell asleep and forgot to tell his wife that we wouldn't be home until twelve. Being screamed at is shaming under any circumstances, but when my future mother-in-law began blasting me, it was downright abusive and humiliating. What made it worse was that even after she learned that I wasn't the cause of her anger, she never apologized for her tirade. I hadn't done anything wrong, but old feelings surfaced, and once again I felt like I had.

Then, shortly after Syd and I were married, I went to a Judaica store to buy a tray for my *Shabbat* (Sabbath) candlesticks. Happy that I found one to match, I showed the tray to my mother-in-law, but didn't get the response I expected. Outraged, she began screaming one of her favorite refrains, something I would hear many times over the course of our relationship: "How could you do such a thing?" followed by, "What's the matter with you, wasting

78

money like that on something so insignificant, when you need more important things!"

On and on she went. I could barely breathe as she raged on about my spending money on something she thought so frivolous. How wrong she was—that tray that I bought over forty-five years ago is one I still use today.

But at that time my anger at being treated so disrespectfully was overshadowed by my shame at having angered my mother-in-law, disappointing her once again. All I wanted to do was share with her, the way I would have with my mother, my excitement at finding the perfect tray. But it seemed no matter what I did—she found fault with it. Thinking back to that time, I realize I didn't stand up for myself because my mother-in-law was only confirming what I already believed: that her anger must have been because of something I did.

The experiences we have during childhood form the patterns for how we see ourselves as adults. Growing up to help us survive in our family of origin, we hide behind masks, donning roles like pleaser, perfectionist, mascot, rebel, hero, and scapegoat that give us our identity. But when the roles become internalized and we get trapped in habitual ways of acting and reacting in the world, then it's a problem. Because by disconnecting from our true selves, we are left with an emptiness inside a mile wide, that no one and nothing can seem to fill, not food, drugs, alcohol, gambling, shopping, or countless other addictions. It doesn't matter how perfect we try to be, how many clothes we buy, degrees we have, or money we amass, feelings of being defective will continue to surface. Working on our dysfunctional history and moving through it is like going on a dig to excavate those disowned parts of ourselves, in order to unearth and reclaim them. It's messy work. But when we do it, and can finally love and accept ourselves, not the way we should be, but the way we are, then we can begin filling up those empty places.

Later on in my journey, when I had an inkling of how much shame I carried, it gave me a greater sense of how much that affected not only how I saw myself, but also why I had such a problem accepting my gay son.

CHAPTER 9

GHOSTS OF THE PAST

...If you don't break your ropes while you are alive,
do you think
ghosts will do it after?
(Kabir)

∽

In 1993, seven years after coming out day, I turned fifty. It was hard to imagine that I was half a century old—and how old that sounded to me. In my head I still felt like a girl, but from time to time my body would give me reminders that I wasn't. But in spite of some aches and pains, fifty was a wonderful birthday for many reasons. For one thing I felt really good about myself and where my life was headed. I was in grad school, excited to be studying a subject I found so thought provoking, and soon my dream of becoming a psychotherapist would be a reality. Another reason was Syd and I were in such a loving place in our relationship. We had grown closer than ever, and later that year we would be celebrating our thirtieth anniversary! On top of that I had made it through Michael's coming out in one piece, happier, more contented, and accepting and there had been times I honestly didn't think that would ever happen.

While I was farther out than I had ever dreamed still I was far from where I wanted to be. In one of my college classes (sociology, I think), the professor said that after a child came out, it took families, on average, seven years to complete their own coming out process. Well, here it was seven years later and that was mostly true —for me at least—with one big exception. No one in our families—Syd's or mine— knew that Michael was gay. We knew we couldn't hide it forever. It was information they'd have to learn sometime, but we kept putting it off.

From the time I was in my early thirties I had been interested in genealogy and had been gathering as much information as I could find about Syd's and my family history. When I became involved in the Holocaust project, I realized just how valuable such information could be, and my interest was peaked. I think I knew intuitively that in order for me to gain some insight into the myriad of feelings I still hadn't resolved, I would have to travel back to the past. I was like a detective trying to figure it all out. Even before I had an interest in psychology (at least consciously), I knew the past held those elusive answers. An interesting quote I once heard by the novelist William Faulkner seemed to explain it, "the past is not dead, it is not even past."

By this time I had compiled a library of family stories, interviews, and audio and video recollections with my mother and sister, and Syd's grandfather and aunt. Syd's mother's stories were conspicuously missing. I had asked Syd's Dad to share some of his recollections, but he had few memories of his child-hood and there was no one in his family left to ask. The interviews came under the guise of practicing for my interviews for the Holocaust Center, or so I thought at the time. Really it was a way for me to gather invaluable information from family members. I would prize them more with each passing year. One of my lasting regrets is that I never interviewed my father; but of course I was only twenty-two when he died and didn't think about such things back then. But one of my father's sisters, my favorite aunt, filled in many of the blanks about his earlier life. And thankfully I had a videotaped interview with my mother. That interview became a link to my own history and gave me a window into my family's gen-erational patterns. As I delved into our stories and personal history, I found the key to open the door to many unanswered questions.

My mother made it easy for me. The video camera was on, but as I began asking her the questions I had neatly written on a yellow legal pad, she hardly even noticed it. She came alive, as she told the wonderfully poignant stories of how our family came to be where and who we are. They were stories I had heard over and over since my childhood, what seemed like a million times, yet I always loved hearing them. But I never fully understood the significance of the stories until years later, after my mother's death, when I listened to our interview again. It was then I was able to connect the dots to what had always been right there, but hidden below the surface.

Like the complexities of my mother's relationship with her mother (*Buba*, I called her—grandmother in Yiddish). *Buba* lived with us and was treated like a queen. My mother idolized her and never had a bad word to say about her. Everyone loved *Buba*— everyone, that is, except me. I honestly don't remember her ever saying a kind word to me. But I do remember how demanding she was of my mother's time and attention. When I first saw the movie, *Brighton Beach Memoirs*, there she was—stern and rigid—so much like my *Buba*.

Buba and *Zeda* (grandfather in Yiddish) worked together in the corner grocery store they owned. They had worked hard and raised four sons and two daughters. When their first granddaughter was a year old, *Buba* found out she was pregnant with my mother. *Zeda* was delighted when my mother was born. His third daughter was his pride and joy—his *mizinka* (baby) he joyfully called her. *Buba* was not. The last thing *Buba* wanted was another child. She was forty, and *Zeda* was fifty-three, not old by today's standards, but way old at the time, and she was highly embarrassed to be having a baby at her age. *Buba* resented having to start over with diapers, feedings, and sleepless nights, and when my mother was born, she had little time or patience for her youngest daughter. To gain a morsel of attention from *Buba*, my mother had to work overtime. One way she did that was by taking on the role of caretaker in her family. Not only did my mother nurse and care for her aging mother and father, but for anyone else in the family who needed caring for. Being a pleaser she learned early on what everyone's needs were. Her own? She didn't even know she had any—unfortunately neither did anyone else. My mother had a heart of gold but over time it would grow tarnished from years of neglecting herself. She took care of everyone else's needs, and then expected my sister and me to take care of hers.

Because she was the "good girl," in her family, the one everyone could depend on; my mother was careful not to do anything that would make waves, that is until she met my father. He was a cook in the Civilian Conservation Corps (CCC) a work relief program for young men from unemployed families during the Great Depression. My father walked into my uncle's produce store in Philadelphia one day, where my mother was the bookkeeper, to buy provisions. They fell in love and because my mother knew her parents would never approve (they refused to believe my father was Jewish), after a short clandestine courtship, she and my father ran away to Elkton, Maryland and were married there. They kept it a secret for a few months, but when *Buba* and *Zeda* found out, it sent shock waves through the family.

The world of my Orthodox grandparents was a small one, with room in it only for what was known and familiar. In their world Jews did not have red hair, blue eyes, and a fair complexion, so to even consider the possibility that my father could be Jewish, was something they couldn't fathom. While he was Jewish to the core, no amount of convincing could prove it by my grandparents. But in time he won them over. Not only could my blue eyed, red-headed father speak perfect Yiddish, he would entertain *Buba* and *Zeda* by singing Hebrew chants as well as their favorite Yiddish songs.

Patterns tend to repeat themselves in families, more often than you might think. Listening to my mother's stories again, there it was, the same pattern, clear as day: to gain her love and attention I took on the role of her caretaker, much like she had done with *Buba*.

There's an old joke in the movie, *Annie Hall*: A guy goes to see a psychiatrist and says, "Doctor, my brother's crazy. He thinks he's a chicken."

The doctor says, "Well why don't you turn him in?"

"I would," the guy says, "but I need the eggs."

Like the guy in the joke, I needed the eggs. Maybe she wasn't the mother I wanted her to be, not many of us get that, but she was a better mother to me than *Buba* had been to her. Likewise, I've been a better mother to Michael and Howard than she was to me. Children don't get much say in who their parents are—we get what we get and none of us are perfect after all. I still had more work to do before I was able to forgive my mother, but I think learning about my family's generational patterns helped that to come about. Still, all these years after her death, I can't imagine that I ever would have told her that Michael was gay.

In the spring of 1993, my mother-in-law invited us, Syd's sister, her husband, their kids and ours to be her guests on a family cruise to celebrate her eightieth birthday. Initially, old fears rose up, and my first thought was not to go. Spending seven days on a cruise ship with my mother-in-law didn't sound like my idea of a good time.

But I mulled it over. On the one hand, it was so out of character; I couldn't help but wonder if this was my mother-in-law's way of reaching out and leaving us with good memories of her. After all, she was eighty years old and had mellowed with age, and a cruise would bring us all together. On the other hand, she had caused me a lot of pain over the years, and had never acknowledged any of it; I still harbored a lot of resentment. Back and forth I went with it, driving myself nuts, until I changed my focus. Putting my wounded ego aside (a novel idea), I looked at my part in keeping our relationship stuck. Okay, I had to admit, I had some culpability here. I checked out years ago, believing there was no hope of anything changing in our relationship, and I wasn't willing to invest any more energy in it. So, with that realization, I made a choice to give it another chance. I would go on the cruise with a loving heart and open mind and see what happened.

One of my favorite self-help books is *Do One Thing Different* by Bill O'Hanlon. It's an easy read that struck a chord with me. O'Hanlon says when we make a change, even a small one, all kinds of things can begin shifting in our lives, and that can create new possibilities. World renowned psychiatrist Milton Erickson (1901–1980) observed that even the smallest behavioral change can set off a domino effect of changes. That certainly was true as it related to the situation with Syd's mother. For a really long time I knew that my mother-in-law was who she was; I couldn't change her. The only thing I could change was the way I looked at the situation. I knew that intellectually, but getting to that place, a short trip—in thought—was not so in reality. That mere twelve inches from my head to my heart took a whole lot longer to travel than I ever imagined.

On the cruise I meditated every day and when I found myself paying attention to the chattering in my head like, "remember when she..."or "yeah but..." I quickly brought my thoughts back into the present.

One morning, not knowing how she might react, I casually asked Syd's mother if she would be willing to let me interview her. By this time my family interviewing project had included just about everyone who was still alive in Syd's and my families except for her, though it was not for lack of trying. In the past, whenever I asked, she would brush me off saying, "I'm not dead yet." So it remained on my list of things to do if ever the opportunity presented itself. But I have to say, I had no expectations that she actually would. When she agreed to the videotaped interview, truthfully, no one was more surprised than me. Having been a Girl Scout, I did come prepared with my yellow legal pad and list of questions just in case. It was slow going at first, but before long she began to relax and open up, and the storyteller in her took over. Soon she was telling story after story, sharing wonderful recollections of her life. When she told what it was like for her when she had polio as a child, it was clear to me how much this experience had affected her, and why she had always been so fearful. This was a story she rarely told, and never in such detail.

My mother-in-law was only two and a half when she was hospitalized with a lung infection. After a few scary days in the hospital she was about to go home. Her parents were celebrating her recovery when the doctor came in with terrible news: she had polio. It was a dreaded diagnosis. Her frightened parents, unsure of what to do, sent her to convalesce at a farm in the country, where there were nurses to massage her legs and lots of fresh air every day. Turned out, the treatment worked; when she left, miraculously, there were no remnants of the polio that sent her there. I had heard this story before, but what I didn't know was how young my mother-in-law had been at the time, and that she was separated from her family for a whole year. For her to be separated from her mother at such a young age would have been terrifying under any circumstances. Now knowing how lonely and frightened she had been without her family, I realized her anger came from her fear, and the way she dealt with the fear was by lashing out at whoever was nearby.

How sad that it took me so long to learn that the woman I had been so frightened of for so many years was herself so frightened, and that her outbursts had little to do with me. How different our relationship might have been if I had figured that out thirty years earlier, but at least I knew it now. I still wasn't ready to tell Syd's mother about Michael. I hadn't gotten there—not yet—Syd either. But at least I was getting closer. The ironic thing was when I let go of my expectations and kept an open heart; our relationship took a whole new direction. Gone were the outbursts (at least those aimed my way), and now she treated me with respect and kindness. It had been a long time coming.

One of the highlights of the cruise was a stop to Jamaica, where Syd and I and our sons went on an outing to Duns River Falls. We did some sightseeing and then climbed the Falls; they were slippery and scary, but, slowly and carefully, I climbed them, pushing through the fear. All along the way, my two precious sons, Michael and Howard, were encouraging me and Syd. When we got into a tight spot, they were right there, to lend a loving hand.

"You can do it, Mom," they assured me. "We're right here."

Indeed they were. Without their help, I doubt I would have made it—climbing the falls or in my greater journey. What an incredible experience it was: great fun, a real adventure, and one of my dearest memories.

The cruise turned out to be a wonderful trip for all of us, especially so for Michael—that's where he met Shawn. When the cruise was over, Michael left for New York, with Shawn, and they've been together ever since.

By listening with awareness to the stories of my mother and Syd's mother, not only did I learn about them, I learned about myself. Looking back into the past helped me find my way into the present, carrying a lot less baggage with me, and so I was able to leave old ghosts behind.

CHAPTER 10

A CHANGE OF HEART

This comes up all the time in mechanical work.
A hang up. You just sit and stare and think,
and search randomly for new information,
and go away and come back again,
and after a while the unseen factors start to emerge.
(Robert M. Pirsig, Zen and the Art of
Motorcycle Maintenance*)*

❧

1994 was a transitional year for us. It had been eight years since coming out day, and big changes were about to take place in our lives. In grad school I had the opportunity to go back into counseling, so I made an appointment to see Dr. Pete Fischer, who had a reputation for being open-minded and empathic. He had a wonderful sense of humor—truly a loving spirit and I always looked forward to our weekly sessions. With Pete's encouragement, I went to my first PFLAG (Parents, Family, and Friends of Lesbians and Gays) meeting. I took a chance and asked Syd to come with me even though we were in very different places—I was pretty much out of the closet—Syd was still way in.

"I'm going to a PFLAG meeting tonight honey, how would you like to come with me?" I asked.

"Are you kidding?" He said. "I wouldn't be caught dead at a PFLAG meeting."

Even though I wasn't thrilled about going alone, I did. The meeting was held at a local church. The twenty-five people who were there were welcoming and put me at ease. I could relate to what many were saying, especially to one woman who, like me, had had a very rough time of it when her daughter came out. After I listened to their stories I felt more comfortable about sharing my own. What I remember most from that first PFLAG meeting was hearing an older couple speak who had three sons—two who were gay. One of them had died of AIDS. After they told their story, heartbreaking and heartwarming all at the same time, they said they came to meetings each month because they wanted to help other parents accept their gay sons and daughters. They were amazing people. I so wished Syd had been there to meet them and share this experience with me. I wondered if we would ever be in a place where we could help other parents like this couple. But from the look of things I doubted that would happen anytime soon.

Up until now when it came to most important issues Syd and I stood together. Sure, we had differences, like every couple, but this was more than that. I was trying to throw open the closet door for all I was worth, and it seemed like Syd was trying his level best to keep it shut tight by ignoring the situation. For the first time in our relationship we were going in completely different directions, drifting further apart, and becoming more and more disconnected from each other. I have to say it was an unfamiliar and troubling feeling. Since the first day we met, Syd has been my closest friend in the world. Now I couldn't reach him and didn't know what to do about it. I confided my frustration to Louise.

"It's not that Syd isn't loving to Michael," I said. "He has been from the beginning, but he's so stuck. It's been over nine years and he still hasn't told anyone about Michael. Here I am trying to get us both out of the closet, but he won't budge. It's almost like he wants to pull me back in with him, and I'll be damned if I'll go back."

Louise listened as I poured out my heart.

"The thing that's so frustrating for me is that Syd thinks things are fine the way the are, and they're so not. He's moving at such a snail's pace, I wonder if he'll ever catch up to me."

"Did it ever occur to you he's moving as fast as he can?" Louise asked. The funny thing was that until that moment, it honestly hadn't. But as soon as I heard Louise's words, I knew she was right. I got it. Syd *was* moving as fast as he could, it just wasn't fast enough for me. I realized he needed to go at his pace, not mine—so I took a step back and allowed Syd the space he needed to be where he was. Michael too had been frustrated with Syd. He was ready to come out to family members, but whenever he broached the subject, Syd would say, "I'm not ready."

"Why don't you think about what you have to do to get ready, Dad?" Michael asked.

When Michael first came out Syd and I would go for long walks, discussing the situation from every angle. After about a year of "massaging the subject to death" as Syd put it, he was ready to move on. He had made peace with Michael being gay, but didn't want to talk about it with anyone. He just wanted to go into his cave and forget about it. That's pretty much what he did. He knew I wasn't done processing and was okay with me telling close friends as long as he didn't know about it from them or from me. There were still issues to sort through, he knew that, but for now, he was done. But after Michael spoke to him, Syd took his words to heart and decided to get ready, he'd go into counseling and confront his issues.

He began seeing Dr. Bob Bollet, a gifted therapist who is not only wise but has great compassion. It turned out Bob's easygoing way and kind heart were just the right fit for him, and with Bob's help, Syd began working his way out of the closet.

Michael remained patient while slowly nudging us along. It didn't escape my notice that he seemed more comfortable and content with himself, especially since going to a weekend growth workshop for gays and lesbians, created by psychologist Dr. Rob Eichberg and David Goodstein, called *The Experience*. When he told me about the workshop I was intrigued. Even though it wasn't for parents with gay children, I thought maybe it could be just the thing Syd and I needed to move each of us to the next level.

"Is the workshop something Dad and I could go to?" I asked Michael. "Do you think we should?"

He answered with a resounding, "Yes. Mom, it would be so amazing. But do you really think Dad would go?"

"Probably not." I admitted. "But I'll ask him anyway."

So I mentioned it to Syd, fully expecting a, "No thanks!" and was almost giddy when he said yes. Silently I said a prayer of thanks for Bob Bollet. In therapy Syd talked to Bob about being unable to move past his fear of coming out. Bob gave him a mental image of trying to walk forward with a rope tied around his waist. The rope was attached to an anchor in the ground that was keeping him stuck and unable to move forward. Bob suggested mentally lifting the anchor out of the ground and throwing it as far in front of himself as he could, and then using the rope to pull himself forward. When Syd made the decision to go to *The Experience*, he said mentally that's what he did, he lifted the anchor of fear keeping him stuck and threw it as far as he could, then literally pulled himself into the fear and then through it. I have to say there was no one more surprised or delighted than me, when two months later there we were, making our way to *The Experience* in Key West.

A few days before we left for the Keys, Syd went to his men's group. He and some of his friends had been meeting once a week for about a year. The group was a safe place for the guys to get together and share what was going on in their lives. When he came home I asked how it went.

"Good," he said. Then added dryly, "I told the guys we were going to Key West for the weekend and I won't be coming home with a tan or a fish." I laughed, as he continued not knowing where he was going with this. "I said we were going to a workshop to learn more about gays and lesbians because Michael is gay."

Whoa! I was absolutely floored. I never expected it. You could have, pardon the cliche, knocked me over with a feather. "What was their reaction?" I asked.

"Everyone was surprised but they were all supportive."

Syd had finally come out big time. He had already moved to the next level, and we hadn't even left town yet.

Driving to the workshop we talked about this adventure we were on and how we felt about it. On the one hand, we were excited to be taking such a big step, but on the other hand, we were uneasy, wondering what we would find when we got there. Sure, we accepted our son, and were willing to stretch, but how far? We weren't so sure of the answer. Michael once gave me some good advice: "When you want to do something, but are more anxious about it than excited, you probably aren't ready to do it. But if you're more excited than anxious, give it a try." We were giving it a try.

After checking into our hotel on Friday, we made our way, somewhat anxiously, to the designated area where the workshop was being held. When we opened the door and saw a group of people who could have been teachers or accountants; we were relieved at how "normal" everyone looked. By the end of the evening, we questioned our judgment about what "normal" looked like. It seemed that, along with our suitcases, we had unwittingly brought other baggage with us as well: our homophobia.

The first night everyone seemed a bit edgy as we settled into our seats. There were mostly men in their early twenties and thirties, some older. About twenty-five per cent were women; all together there were about sixty people. With the exception of one other mother, we were the only parents. The facilitator did introductions and gave us the schedule for the weekend. The next two days would be spent doing a variety of exercises and activities geared toward discarding self-imposed limitations, becoming more self-accepting, and gaining self-confidence. One goal of the weekend, quite a lofty one I thought, was that people who had not already come out to their families would be ready to do so by Sunday.

Saturday, we began the day feeling more at ease and happy to be there. Everyone was welcoming, although somewhat surprised to have parents at their workshop. One of the first people we met was Bill, a man in his late forties, who had just lost his life partner of twenty-five years six weeks earlier. After his partner's death, Bill, crushed that his parents had never accepted or even acknowledged their relationship, asked his parents to send flowers to the funeral; they wouldn't do it, even when Bill offered to pay for them. All he wanted from his parents was some small recognition of his twenty-five year relationship, and they wouldn't even give him that. Dealing with the pain of losing his beloved partner, Bill looked to his family for solace. But, instead, they were the cause of more heartache for him. Syd and I knew that these things happened, but this was the first time we actually met someone it had happened to. Many of the people we met had similar stories.

While some had close relationships with their families, more than a few told us how their families abandoned them when they came out.

"It's bad enough we have to deal with society's rejection and hatred," they told us, "But being abandoned by our own families—how are we supposed to deal with that?"

The people who had the hardest time coming out were from strict Christian backgrounds. Pummeled with Biblical passages about abomination, they were told they would go to hell. One young man who was disowned by his parents after he came out said, "How can I be an abomination today when yesterday I was the golden boy?" How I wished I had an answer. Suddenly, Syd and I began waking up to the complexity and uncertainty involved in coming out, a process much more difficult than we ever imagined.

As the weekend progressed, we became stand-in parents for the group, and soon parental issues were called the "Enid and Syd process." We were asked many questions, such as, "How did you feel when you found out Michael was gay? How long did it take til you were okay with it? How do you feel about Michael now?" Since a lot of people planned to come out to their parents after the weekend, we were asked what was "the right way," the most loving way to do it? How could they make the process as painless for their parents as possible, and what kind of response could they expect? This was all so new for us. I came to the workshop with more questions than answers, and it was unnerving to me that *they* thought *we* had the answers.

There is a saying, "In the valley of the blind, the one-eyed man is king," which I suppose was as good a description of us that weekend as any. So we spoke from our own experience, saying that as far as we knew there was no painless way to do it. At best, they could pick the right setting, perhaps the right moment, but we didn't know of any approach that would make it painless. We explained that what made it especially hard was there was no way of knowing or predicting how people's parents might react, since everyone sees things through the lens of their own experience. We were prime examples of that.

By the end of the first day, I understood the angst of coming out. There was so much at stake—the risk of losing a parent's love was huge. For many the risk was too great, and they chose to stay closeted. For the first time, I grasped how hard it must have been for Michael to come out to us, and painfully, I saw how self-absorbed I had been, and how little thought I gave to what it was like for him to tell us. His coming out had been all about *me*. When Michael so desperately needed loving parents, we weren't there for him. He had to deal with all his questions, fears and concerns about being gay alone. When the impact of that hit me, guilt, my least favorite emotion, visited. Memories came flooding back of that night in our family room almost ten years earlier. How Michael struggled to tell us, knowing the inevitability of the hurt we would feel, and how crushed he had been by our reaction. Say what you will about guilt, it opened my eyes. After spending the weekend with a roomful of people who, much like Michael, made the discovery that they were gay, finally it became clear to me. If sexual orientation was a choice, none of the people we met would have chosen it, or all the pain that came along with it.

That weekend, we were witnesses, as people shared their pain, their struggle, their warmth—themselves, and we felt privileged to affirm them and be a part of their lives, even for just a weekend. At the beginning of my journey, I couldn't understand why Michael had the need to tell us about his sexual orientation. Now I realized how much love and trust it took for him to share this part of his life with us, and how lucky we were that he knew our love for him was strong enough to withstand his coming out—even though for quite a while it was an uphill climb.

I was missing him so and wished he were with us. I couldn't wait to see him and talk about the weekend, and all we were learning. There were so many things I wanted to tell him.

Here is a piece I wrote in my journal, the last day of the workshop:

The men and women we've met here are in so much pain. They've been deeply wounded by the people they love the most—As I become more open and aware, I know it's time for me to help other parents with gay children going through the coming out process. I hoped to find answers here—so far I haven't. Like how do we deal with the homophobia? society? fear? How do we break through the shame? How grateful I am that Syd is with me on this journey. His impact has been amazing. So many people told us, I might get my mother to come to this workshop—but my father—never.

At the end of the weekend there was a graduation. All the participants stood in a circle, eyes closed, singing and swaying to the song, "The Rose," written by Amanda McBroom and sung by Bette Midler. As I focused on the meaning between the lines, the message was clear: what's important is to live the life you have, that staying in the closet is a kind of death, and that the pain of coming out can be a catalyst for new growth to unfold.

> *...It's the heart afraid of breaking,*
> *that never learns to dance.*
> *It's the dream afraid of waking,*
> *that never takes the chance.*
> *It's the one who won't be taken,*
> *who cannot seem to give,*
> *and the soul afraid of dying,*
> *that never learns to live.*
> *When the night has been too lonely,*
> *and the road has been too long,*
> *and you think that love is only*
> *for the lucky and the strong,*
> *just remember in the winter,*
> *far beneath the bitter snows,*
> *lies the seed that with the sun's love,*
> *in the spring, becomes the rose.*[4]

My heart was full—we had touched many lives, but even more, our own lives had been touched, profoundly. As I stood in the circle, caught up in

---

[4] "The Rose" by Amanda McBroom. Copyright © TKTK. International Copyright Secured. All Rights Reserved. Used by Permission.

the moment, I felt something stir in front of me. Instinctively, I opened my eyes. There stood Michael standing before us filled with love and gratitude, holding a long-stemmed red rose. What a moment it was of indescribable connection and understanding! Stunned and weeping, I embraced him. Knowing this weekend would open our minds as well as our hearts, Michael flew down to be part of the graduation ceremony, as others had done for their family members.

Those of us there that weekend left with a sense of peace with ourselves and a deeper understanding of who we were. For me it was transformational really. Because now it was no longer just about one of my sons, but about all the sons and daughters who had no one to speak up for them, or to support them. I shifted into a whole new place in my relationship with Michael and in my relationship with the gay community. Driving home with Michael we processed the weekend, talking about what we learned. Syd and I shared some of the life-changing stories we heard, and we brainstormed where we would go from here. The gay community desperately needed champions. We knew a way for us to make a difference was to step up and become involved.

We talked about facilitating a future workshop like *The Experience* that would be for parents with gay children, but were to find that was a whole lot easier said than done. But really what mattered to me was not so much what Syd and I would do, or how we would do it, but that we were together in whatever it was. A few weeks later I went to another PFLAG meeting this time with Syd and there we found a place to help other parents going through the many feelings that come along with having a gay child. In some families parents become very polarized about having a gay child and the marriage is not able to sustain itself. How grateful I was that Syd and I found our way back to each other.

One morning a short time later, Syd handed me a bulletin from GLBCC, the Gay, Lesbian and Bisexual community center in Orlando. They were asking for volunteers to serve on their Board of Directors.

"You said you want to be more active in the gay community," Syd said. "Here's your opportunity."

I took it and served on the Board of GLBCC for several years, and also on the Board of PFLAG with Syd. At meetings he often tells parents his response when I asked him to go to a PFLAG meeting for the first time—"I wouldn't be caught dead at a PFLAG meeting." Most parents know the feeling. I think it gives them some comfort knowing it's possible to go from "no way" to serving on the Orlando PFLAG Board.

Going to *The Experience* made me aware of the struggle gay people faced, and I felt the need to do something, no matter how small, to change things. Being a straight ally was one way to accomplish that.

CHAPTER 11

TAKING CARE OF FAMILY BUSINESS

The little reed bending with the force of wind,
soon stood upright again when the storm had passed.
(Aesop)

∽

A few months after *The Experience*, Michael was in Miami and went to visit his grandmother. With Syd's blessing and mine, he planned to tell her that he was gay. He was sure the news wouldn't change anything between them. She had always been there for him in the past, and he felt sure she would be there for him now. He was certainly right about that.

"Darling," she said. "I already knew; I've known for a long time, and it makes no difference to me. I love you and always will."

Any anxiety Michael might have felt was instantly lifted, and he continued. "I met someone special, Grandma, and I think he's the one."

"Is it that blond from the cruise?" She asked.

"It is," Michael said, with some surprise.

"When I saw the two of you together, I had a feeling about it," she said.

How interesting we thought, when Michael told us about their conversation, that she had made that connection.

Later when they went out for dinner, she met Shawn and was warm and accepting without a trace of judgment. When Syd and I spoke with her about it, she seemed content that Michael was settled and happy in a committed relationship. What did concern her though was how difficult Michael's coming out must have been for us. What I learned was that under her tough exterior, my mother-in-law had a most loving heart, and a great capacity for love, something her grandchildren had known from the day they were born. Too bad she kept it so hidden from her children and from me for so many years.

Life keeps moving on in what seems like continuing cycles, as we go from beginnings to endings and then back again. One of those endings came less than two years after Syd's mother's eightieth birthday cruise, when her health began to fail and she died after a short illness. Her death came after she and I had tied up many of the loose threads that for so many years kept us separated. I was grateful that our relationship, once so rocky, had become harmonious and much healthier. I found that the old resentments I felt toward her had melted away, and in my heart what remained was forgiveness, affection, and a real appreciation for the loving presence she played in the lives of my children.

Syd and I went to Miami and were making plans for his mother's funeral when Michael called asking if it would be okay with us for Shawn to come with him. It was an uncomfortable situation for Syd; he didn't feel right about it. There would be old friends and family members we rarely saw at the funeral, who didn't even know Michael was gay, let alone that he had a partner. Syd didn't think his mother's funeral was the time or place for Michael to be coming out, and because he felt strongly about it, I wanted to honor his wishes. It was, after all his mother's funeral. So we told Michael no, and felt terrible—all of us did. After Syd and I discussed it, we knew we had to set things right, so we wouldn't find ourselves in a situation where Shawn was excluded from anything in our family again.

So after the funeral, during *Shiva* (the Jewish mourning period when friends and family come to visit, bring food, and tell stories), Michael broke the news to close family members. When Michael told his godmother and his great aunt, they said they had loved him since the day he was born and that would never change. He was still Michael. When Syd and I told a friend about Michael, he confided to us that his brother was gay and that when he came out their parents had disowned him. He felt his brother's life would have been very different if his parents had been as open-minded as we were. Everyone was accepting, I don't think the news was a big shock, and if anyone did have any qualms about it, they kept it to themselves. We all breathed a sigh of relief. When everyone left, Syd said, "Today we settled all family business," and we laughed at his reference to the line from *The Godfather*. It was finally done and it felt like a huge weight had been lifted. We were OUT.

Ironically, it solved a problem we would have had to face in a few months anyway, one that we had been unsure how to resolve. In the fall Howard and his fiancée Liz were getting married, and we didn't know how to deal with the gay issue at the wedding. We wanted all eyes to be on the bride and groom, not on Michael and Shawn. In today's world it wouldn't be such a big deal, but in the mid-1990s it was. So that everything would go smoothly at the wedding, Syd and I had decided we wanted to tell close friends and family before the event. The big question was how. After the cruise, we joked about our "how to tell everyone before the wedding" problem. Maybe we could put a note in the wedding invitation saying, "Oh, and by the way"...or how about doing an early holiday letter in July, slipping in the news that, "oops, we forgot to mention it, but Michael came out to us ten years ago"? We were having fun with it, but it was a real dilemma. Now, because of Syd's mother's death and the conversations during *Shiva*, it was taken care of and we didn't have to worry about anything detracting from Howard and Liz's big day.

Since I didn't expect my sister or her family to come from Israel for the wedding, I felt there was no need to tell her. Never very close, we had drifted apart since our mother's death and rarely spoke. But, after she got the invitation, my sister wrote saying she and her husband were coming to the wedding. I have to say I was surprised that they'd make the trip from Israel. But weddings are filled with hope and possibility that can bring families together; I was happy ours was bringing my sister and brother-in-law to share the occasion. So that meant telling her the news before they got here. Michael volunteered to make the phone call.

"It went very well," he said later, after they spoke. "Honest, Mom, it was no biggie. She said she suspected I was gay, and it doesn't matter to her at all. She told me she loves me no matter what."

Another door opened.

Later, my sister called, hurt that I hadn't told her.

"I can't believe that you didn't tell me." She said. "Why? You know better than anyone that I've always been open minded and tolerant. Even back in college I had gay friends. Did you think it would matter to me? Or that it would change the way I feel about Michael? Let me assure you, it doesn't matter at all."

I told her I was happy to know how she felt, that it meant a lot to me that she was so accepting and loving to Michael. But this wasn't something we could discuss on the phone. I thought it would be best to talk about it after the wedding. She agreed.

So when all the festivities were over, Michael, my sister, and I sat down in my living room for a conversation that would be up close and personal. No small talk here. My intention was to be very honest about my reasons for not telling her, and I gave a lot of thought to what I would say, and how I could say it in a loving way. I didn't know how my sister might react, but it was an exchange that was long overdue.

"The reason I didn't tell you," I said, "didn't have to do with Michael. It was because of our relationship. When Michael came out, I was so emotionally fragile and raw, with such a confusion of feelings, I could not have handled being hurt or judged in any way. Growing up, you had hurt me too many times, and too many times when I needed you in the past, you weren't there for me."

My sister sat and listened. There were no defensive explanations, or interruptions. She just listened.

"When Michael came out," I went on, "the fabric of my life unraveled, and everything fell apart. I was vulnerable, terrified, and deeply depressed. I felt like a complete failure as a mother."

While I spoke, my sister glanced at Michael several times, and I could tell she was concerned that my words would be hurtful to him. But Michael knew that though I had felt that way once, I didn't feel that way now. Now I was being real. And as I shared with my sister how Michael's coming out affected my life, she honestly listened to me with the ears of her heart. She wept as I spoke and later we had a heartfelt hug.

"I'm sorry that you went through so much pain," she said lovingly.

Since the time we were children, my sister and I had built high walls around ourselves, to keep each other out. In our home anger was an emotion we were not allowed to express—at least not to any of the adults in our lives, not that we didn't feel it. We felt it, all right, and took it out on each other. Our rows and bickering only escalated over the years. In the drama we were playing ours were model parents—and we were just two sisters who couldn't get along. Because our parents lived so unconsciously they allowed our constant fighting to go on. How wonderful it felt to dismantle the walls for a rare moment of intimacy and closeness.

When Michael and Shawn were vacationing in the Middle East a few years later, they stayed with my sister, brother-in-law and their family and were warmly welcomed by all.

So how was it, I wondered, and you might be too, that more than a few of our relatives knew or suspected that Michael was gay, and we were unable to see, what seemed so visible to them? When Michael first came out he was very closeted, keeping his sexual orientation from all but his closest friends. As time went by he became less guarded. He no longer even pretended to be dating, and now there were guys around him instead of girls. I suppose close family members began noticing the changes and suspected he might be gay. A cousin used to say that it's not a good idea to ask a question that you don't want to know the answer to. Well, neither Syd nor I was asking any questions. Of course now I know why. I was in denial. There is a saying that the mother is the first to know and the last to find out. Had there been signs? Sure, but I didn't want to see them, so I didn't, and like the first snow, they quickly dissolved. When a doubt or thought about Michael's sexual orientation drifted into my mind, quickly I brushed it under that proverbial rug. As long as I stayed unconscious, I could see things the way I wanted them to be, instead of the way they were.

Like many parents with a gay child, Syd and I had no way of knowing how our family members would react to the news that Michael was gay, and because there's really no way to gauge it, that only added to the anxiety of coming out. The best we could do was to make an educated guess. So that made coming out to our families a little like holding out our hand to what we hoped would be a friendly dog, not knowing if it would lick our hand, or bite it.

I think another big fear many parents have that's often overlooked in coming out—is using the word "homosexual" to describe your child. It's a word that's not only charged with fear, it has layer upon layer of shame attached to it. For so many of us, just hearing "that word" can conjure up any number of false assumptions—think about all the expressions that pop into your mind when you hear it. But here's what I lost sight of—when "that word" has a face, and the face is attached to someone you love, someone you've watched grow up and loved all of his life, things start looking very different. A faceless stranger can be judged and treated with contempt, but one of your own? Not so easy, especially when you know their story. When I figured out that "homosexual" was only a word and my fear of it was irrational, the fear soon dissipated.

There's a story I heard about how fear can keep us imprisoned in old patterns. It's by John O'Donahue, an Irish philosopher, and is about a man condemned to spend a night in prison with a poisonous snake. The man knew he must remain perfectly still; that if he made even the slightest movement, the snake would strike and likely kill him. All that night the man stood terrified in the corner of his cell, not moving a muscle, so he wouldn't alert the snake to his presence. At the first light of dawn the man could make out the shape of the snake in the opposite corner of the room. "God, wasn't I lucky that I didn't snore or make any movement," he said to himself. But as more light came into the room, the man saw that what was in the opposite corner wasn't a snake at all, but rather it was merely a large piece of rope. How many times in our lives have we been afraid of the irrational snakes in our lives, when in reality they were just harmless ropes lying about in one of the many rooms of our mind?

So after all the hours of anxiety spent worrying about coming out to our families—it was done and we had survived in spite of a harmless rope or two along the way. Finally, the drama of it was over, and Syd and I were so ready to move on and focus on other things.

CHAPTER 12

FINDING MY VOICE

Love begins when we set aside all of our masks.
We need to forget how it was and see how it is.
Life is an experience, not an explanation.
(Yogi Amit Desai)

᠙

In my last semester of graduate school, I took a required class in human sexuality. The first night of the class while looking over the syllabus, I saw there was a section on sexual orientation; a panel of gay men and women was scheduled to speak to the class and then answer people's questions. That was both intriguing and uncomfortable for me. Intriguing because hearing gay people speak about their experience could be a way to open people's minds; uncomfortable because no one at school knew I had a gay son; it had never felt safe to tell anyone. I flirted with the idea that if things went well, I might take the opportunity to come out during that class. But as the date for the panel discussion was approaching, I found myself becoming very anxious about it. There were about fifty students in the class, all about to become mental health or school counselors.

So I tried to quiet my fears, assuring myself that, after all, who would be more accepting than a roomful of counselors? But no matter how many times I told myself the outcome would be positive, my intuition kept telling me otherwise.

The night finally arrived. My professor introduced the four-member panel of two men and two women to the class and each person told their story. I listened with growing admiration for the way they had each overcome the struggle of coming out, first to themselves, and then to their families. After discovering they were gay, each of them had gone into therapy, and credited counseling with helping them come to a place of acceptance with their sexual orientation. So far, so good, I thought. Who wouldn't be inspired by hearing real stories of how therapy made a difference in people's lives—especially people about to be counselors?

But then the questions began. Boy, had my intuition been right! I sat in disbelief as my classmates, Master's level students, months away from graduation, began asking the most unbelievably inappropriate questions. Was it true, they asked, that gays coerced and lured young people to have sex? What was it, they wanted to know, that gay people did to "convert" others to become gay? Did they really think having anal sex was *normal*? That was only the half of it. I was stunned by the questions and comments. They were disrespectful, cheeky, and so over the line that it sounded like the students were deliberately trying to denigrate the people on the panel. I looked around the room, rife with homophobia, and literally felt sick to my stomach. You couldn't call their comments ignorant, there's a thin line between ignorance and stupidity; my classmates had crossed that line.

The evening continued spiraling downward, and I thought how different my life might be today, if I had gone into therapy with one of these soon to be counselors. I shuttered at the thought of how much damage they might do out in the world. Silently, I said a prayer of thanks for my counselors Hedy Schleiffer and Pete Fischer, for being nonjudgmental and accepting; making them polar opposites of my classmates. When I looked around the room, I saw along with my own, a few other disbelieving faces. By all rights, I was far enough along in my journey that I should have stood up and challenged the homophobic comments. If I had, others might have joined me, and that could have made a difference. But it was only in my head I was shouting, "Do you hear what you're saying? What could you be thinking? And *you* are going to be *counselors?*"

But instead of letting them know how appalled I was, and that they didn't speak for me; I sat there in silence, as though I was glued to my chair. How did that happen? Later, dissecting the evening, I realized this was the first time that I had ever been in an environment this hostile, and I felt, not only intimidated, but also outnumbered. In the face of such blatant bigotry, old insecurities surfaced, and I was at a loss to defend my views. My professor allowed the questions to continue, even after they had passed the point of no return; for what reason, I couldn't imagine. But after the panel had gone, I could see that she, as well as several other classmates, were as disgusted as I was by the class's bigotry.

Just as I was asking myself, "What on earth would they do if a gay client came to see them for counseling?" my professor turned to those who had been so vocal and asked them that very question.

"I wouldn't see anyone gay. I'd refer them to someone else," someone said, and others nodded.

"And suppose a client came to see you because they were conflicted with having a gay family member? How would you deal with that?" she asked.

The response: refer them.

Continuing to probe, my professor asked, "Suppose a client had a sexually transmitted disease? Or had been unfaithful to their partner? Then what would you do?"

My classmates seemed to be on a roll. To each question the response was: refer them to someone else. More than a few of my classmates said that seeing such people would go against their faith.

"So when you hang up your shingle, what will your signboard say? 'Psychotherapy: No Gays, No Sexually Transmitted Diseases, No Infidelity'?"

Many of the students nodded in agreement.

"What I'm wondering," she asked rhetorically, "is what kind of a practice you think you'll have?" She paused and said, "Allow me to answer that for you: a very small one. If you only want to see those people with your values and belief systems, you're in the wrong profession."

Indeed, they were. Their comments said a whole lot more about them than about the panel members.

What I found especially interesting was that the issues they had such difficulty with were not only homosexuality, but with sexuality in general. Sadly, I learned that a lot of my classmates in this master's-level counseling program were no different from a lot of people in mainstream society. The thought of them out in the world as counselors was a scary and sobering one.

I left class feeling a sense of hopelessness and anger, mostly directed at myself. Even though I had come so far along on my journey, I wondered how I could have gone so far off course, and been so intimidated, that I had kept silent while the men and women on the panel were being lampooned with insulting questions from my classmates. Even when our professor confronted the class with the reality of what it is to become a counselor, they showed no regret for their behavior, nor did they think they had been out of line.

The thing about coming out is it's not a one-time thing; it's more like crossing a series of bridges, littered with roadblocks obstructing the way. I had to figure out how to get past this one—it was a biggie. But one thing I knew for sure: I would not sit back in the face of such homophobia and remain silent again.

In my next counseling session with Pete, I told him about the evening and he shook his head in disbelief. He encouraged me to be more proactive. It was a direction I wanted to take, but wondered if I was ready to begin speaking out about homophobia and homosexuality to people whose beliefs might very well be like those of my classmates. In school I had done a fair share of speaking on a variety of subjects, but speaking so personally about my life and family was a whole different story. I wasn't sure I was up to the task. But after giving it a lot of thought, I knew it was something I had to do—and that somehow I would find a way to do it.

In the spring of 1996 I completed graduate school. Finally I had my degree in Mental Health Counseling and in a few months I'd be out in the world working as a therapist. How sweet it was to have reached my goal! Now before starting work, I was cleaning up some of the clutter around my house that had accumulated during my last semester of school. Sorting through neglected piles of papers, magazines, and unread mail, I was making my way through a large stack of articles. I glanced over one to see if it was something I wanted to read or toss, when my eyes fell on a quote by Joseph Campbell. His words seemed to jump off the page and drop in front of me like scenery descending for the next act in a play. As it happened a new act actually was about to begin, and only moments later as I read, and then re-read Campbell's comment:

"When we place our ladder against the wall of other people's expectations, we are bound to fail. For even if we scale the wall, when we get to the top, where are we?"

Something clicked and I was transported by Campbell's words. The answer was a simple one: it's where someone else wants us to be. Ironically it was an insight I had several times before, but had trouble remembering. Why now did I get it? I think when you're on a spiritual journey, simple concepts often get lost. It's part of the growth process. There's a saying that when the student is ready, the teacher appears. Campbell's words came at a moment in time when I was open to hearing them, and they were said in a way I hadn't heard before. It was like looking through a kaleidoscope, and with a simple turn of the wheel, a lifelong pattern suddenly came together, and was unmistakably clear. I was still perched on that wall of other people's expectations, still fearful of what other people thought of me, and that fear was what kept me from speaking out during that human sexuality class fiasco. But after reading Campbell's words, just like that, in an instant, I didn't care what other people thought of homosexuality—or of me—it didn't matter. Who were these other people, anyway? And what did their thoughts or judgments have to do with me, or my family? Nothing, nada, zilch. Let them think what they wanted. That wasn't my business.

Of course the powers that be threw down the gauntlet on that pronouncement to put me to the test. A few days after this epiphany, I was out shopping for a pair of shoes; when I found the ones I wanted, I went to the counter to pay for them. A woman was waiting in front of me impatiently looking at her watch, while the two of us stood in line listening to the conversation the clerk was having on the phone. It went something like this:

"Well I won't put up with it. Who do those gays think they are? John wants to invite some gay kid to his graduation party, but I told him that's not happening. I don't want him having anything to do with those people. That's how it starts."

Then, seeing there were customers waiting, she said a hasty goodbye and hung up the phone. "Gays," the clerk said with disgust, shaking her head.

The woman in front of me nodded her agreement.

Well here it is I thought, my heart pounding, the time to say something.

When I got to the register, the clerk, still hot under the collar, said to me, "I don't know what the world is coming to—gays think they have the right to do whatever they want. If you ask me, they should stay in the closet where they belong."

"You seem to have an issue with gay people," I said. "Why do you think that is?"

"What do you mean?" she retorted. "I don't have an issue with gay people."

She must have assumed I would feel the same way she did. After all the woman in front of me did, and I guessed most everyone else she knew did too.

"I have a gay son," I said. "He just wants the same rights and opportunities your son has. And I don't think anyone belongs in a closet, whether they're gay or straight." The woman was speechless as I went on. "You really shouldn't assume that everyone feels the same way that you do. You're entitled to your opinion, but do you really think it's appropriate for you to be voicing it in a business setting, when it's very possible that you could be offending someone by your comments?"

It wasn't a rhetorical question, but the clerk didn't answer. So, I paid for the shoes and left, with a silent thank you to Joseph Campbell. I felt incredibly liberated.

After this incident I decided it was time to call my human sexuality professor. When I told her I'd like to represent a mother's perspective on her next gay and lesbian panel, she welcomed the idea. And so at this presentation I was in the classroom, not as a closeted student, this time I was there as a therapist and guest speaker. I didn't expect to change the world. What I did expect was that I'd be treated with respect, and that what happened in the last class would not happen in this one. How I'd accomplish it I wasn't sure, but I was determined that this evening would have a very different outcome. I began with a favorite Zen story:

There was a learned professor of oriental studies who visited a very famous Zen master in the Orient. The master received the professor in his private room. As soon as the professor seated himself, he talked on and on about Zen philosophy, while the master said nothing.

The professor continued talking until finally, the master said, "let us have tea," and he began pouring tea into his guest's cup. The professor, so busy talking, hardly noticed. But suddenly the professor jumped to his feet when he realized that the Zen master was still pouring tea, even though the cup had long since overflowed, and the tea was spilling out onto the tatami mat in front of them. And still the master continued pouring.

"Stop, stop, what are you doing?" cried the professor. "Can't you see the cup is already filled to the top and the tea is spilling all over the tatami mat?"

The master looked up, "Just as this cup cannot hold any more tea when it is already filled," he said, "how can you be taught anything when your mind is overflowing, much like this teacup?"

I waited a moment for the impact of the story to sink in.

"I know many of you are here with a teacup full of your own understanding and beliefs about homosexuality," I said. "But I'd like to ask you to put your beliefs up on the shelf for the next few moments. If you need them, they'll be there for you to gather up when you leave. For now, I'd like to invite you to listen—with an empty cup."

I glanced around the room and waited until I had everyone's attention. When I did, I told the story of Michael's coming out, and how, like so many people, I too had prejudice toward gays—prejudice that I hadn't even been aware of—until it affected me personally. When I asked if anyone had any questions, the ones I got were probing and curious. Some of the questions they asked were if I thought being gay was a choice, how long it took until I accepted my son, and how I felt about gay people now. The students were respectful, supportive, and surprised, I think, to know I had a gay son, and that I was willing to speak so candidly about it. I felt hopeful that I had opened a few minds at least, and given some insight into the complexity of coming to terms with issues of sexual orientation for both parents and children. On the way to my car as I left the class that night,

I remember thinking, it was a start. This human sexuality presentation was nothing like the last one. I achieved what I hoped. Driving home, I felt a great sense of relief, as well as accomplishment.

When Syd and I saw Hedy at a party a short time later she told us about a couple's workshop that she and her husband Yumi attended called *Getting the Love you Want* (GTLYW), offered by Imago Relationships. "It's very safe, especially for men," Hedy told us. "You both get to do your own internal process, and then the work you do is with each other." What piqued my interest about it was her comment, "It's a way to use your relationship for personal growth and to learn new communication skills."

I was all for going. The biggest surprise was that Syd was the one who said, "Let's do it." So after we checked it out, we signed up to go. During the workshop we went vertically into our relationship where we saw the origin of our patterns, how they affected our relationship, and the way we related to each other. The mirroring process we learned to do that weekend has been a tool we've used many times over the years to resolve conflicts and troublesome issues. At the end of the weekend we had a greater understanding of the cause of our conflicts, and a depth of love that I had only dreamed of having. I also had a greater understanding of the role parents' play in their children's lives. I remembered reading a poem years earlier by Khahil Gibran from *The Prophet* that had touched a chord in me. Now I understood it from a much deeper place.

*And a woman who held a babe against
her bosom said, Speak to us of Children.
And he said:
Your children are not your children.
They are the sons and daughters of Life's longing
for itself.
They come through you but not from you,
And though they are with you yet they belong
not to you.
You may give them your love but not your
thoughts,
For they have their own thoughts.
You may house their bodies but not their souls,
For their souls dwell in the house of tomorrow,
which you cannot visit, not even in your dreams.
You may strive to be like them, but seek not to
make them like you.
For life goes not backward, nor tarries with
yesterday.
You are the bows from which your children as
living arrows are sent forth.
The archer sees the mark upon the path of
the infinite,
and He bends you with his might
that His arrows may go swift and far.
Let your bending in the archer's hand be for
gladness;
For even as He loves the arrow that flies,
so He loves also the bow that is stable.*

I had demanded so much of my children, and owning the mistakes I made raising them was extremely painful for me. Not long ago I was reading the book by Khaled Husseini, *The Kite Runner*, and stumbled onto a line that best describes it: "Children aren't coloring books; you don't get to fill them with your favorite colors." It hadn't been enough for me that my sons be who they were; I wanted them to be who *I* wanted them to be. I knew how important it was for me to share that understanding with them; they needed to know it too. So I spoke first to Michael, then to Howard. I told each of them how dearly I loved them, how sorry I was for the mistakes I made over the years. I explained where some of my patterns came from, and asked them to forgive me for any hurt I caused them. If I could, I told them I would gladly turn back the clock and do it over again—better and smarter this time. Both my sons were incredibly loving and forgiving. Since that time we have been forging new, healthier relationships, and for that, I am eternally grateful.

And so I was able to let go of the way my children were *supposed* to be, and accept and embrace who they were. I gave them back their lives, so they could live their own dreams, and I took responsibility for living my own.

Now that I was speaking out more, sometimes it felt like I was flying without a net. I wanted to learn different ways to handle uncomfortable situations. Soon help was on the way when Syd and I got a brochure about a two-day workshop being held in Tampa called, "Speaking Out Against Homophobia." Warren Blumenfield, a noted author, activist and educator, was leading the workshop. We decided to go. As soon as we walked in the door, I knew we were in the right place. The workshop was experiential, educational and enriching, aimed at helping us counter homophobia and prejudice against sexual minorities in our communities, and within ourselves.

The weekend was a real learning experience on many levels. For example, before the workshop, I had no real understanding of what transgender meant, but learned that people who identify as transgendered have a sense of themselves as male or female that's opposite from their birth sex. Later I would learn more about it when I met transgendered people through PFLAG and at Warren's next workshop. We were educating ourselves and stretching, and as we did Syd and I found our world expanding.

Because Warren's workshop was so powerful for us, Syd and I arranged for him to come to Orlando to give the workshop here. It too, was a success, and before it concluded about a dozen of us formed a speaker's bureau. When a gay friend and I went to speak at a college sociology class, I didn't think I had any remnants of homophobia left, but soon learned otherwise. Each of us briefly told our respective stories, and after we had spoken, someone asked, "Did you ever suspect your son might be gay before he came out to you?"

"No," I replied. "He didn't look or act gay, so I never thought much about it."

My friend challenged me. "Enid, did you hear how stereotypical your comment was?"

I was taken aback. He was right. I hadn't even realized it, but I was perpetuating the old myth that there are obvious ways that all gay people "look" or "act."

At first I felt a rush of shame for my comment, but then took a deep breath and said, "There you go. What you just heard was a perfect example of internalized homophobia, and I should know better. It's true that some gay men are effeminate, but many, like my son, are not."

My comment made for an interesting way to explain and examine the stereotypical ways many of us look at gay people.

I knew speaking out meant I'd be exposed to people who saw the world differently than I did. But I wasn't about to let that stand in my way of doing it. I spoke at college classes, community organizations, and company diversity awareness groups, and I held my own. And as I did, I began to notice a different level of understanding and acceptance of gay people in the groups I spoke to. It seemed that it wasn't only times that were changing; so were people. Hadn't we spent enough time living in fear and hatred? Wasn't it time to accept one another regardless of our differences?

CHAPTER 13

COMMITMENT

The sun brings forth the beginning
the moon holds it in darkness
As above, so below
For there is no greater magic in all the world
than that of people joined together in love.
(Wiccan Blessing)

༄

When Michael introduced me to Shawn, who was working in the purser's office on the family cruise we took in 1995, there was something about him aside from his good looks that I was drawn to. Not only was he warm and engaging, my intuition told me that he had a good heart. It turned out I was right about that. I would have had to be blind not to see the attraction between the two of them, but honestly, I didn't think it was anything more than a casual shipboard romance. About that, I was wrong. When the cruise ended, we all said our goodbyes and headed for our respective homes. To my surprise Michael and Shawn left together, and the next thing I knew, Shawn had moved to New York and into Michael's apartment. Syd and I never expected the relationship to last. They were from such different backgrounds; Shawn was brought up in a Christian home, Michael a Jewish one, and they didn't seem to have much in common. But after a few months we realized that though their relationship started out as a chance encounter, it was growing into something much deeper.

Like most parents, what Syd and I wanted for our children was for them to find loving partners, settle down, and begin their own families. That had happened for Howard, who was by this time happily married to Liz, a beautiful redhead with the most loving heart. We were thrilled to have such a wonderful daughter-in-law we all loved and who was such a doll at that. We so wanted the same for Michael, but because he was gay we doubted that would ever happen—and had long since reconciled to it.

But that changed when Shawn came on the scene. By the time he and Michael had been together for a year, Syd and I thought of Shawn as a part of our family, and we were genuinely happy when they told us they planned to spend the rest of their lives together. Like any other couple, they wanted to acknowledge and validate their relationship, and they decided to have a commitment ceremony, since they couldn't have a legal one. It was a bold move at the time, quite unconventional.

Syd and I were excited about it, but we had some concerns and, like Tevye in *Fiddler on the Roof,* we went back and forth with it. On the one hand we knew how good-hearted, caring, and devoted Shawn was to Michael. On the other hand, we also knew life could be difficult enough as a same-sex couple, let alone an interfaith one. We wondered how they would bridge that gap, in my eyes it was a big one. We gave it a lot of thought and after boiling our soup full of concerns down into a bouillon cube, what became clear was that Michael and Shawn would work through any issues that came along, just like Syd and I, or any other couple would do. They were making a commitment to each other to do just that. The bottom line—it wasn't our decision. It was Michael's and Shawn's and they would figure it all out.

But there was one thing that was troubling me. For any other couple beginning a life together, there would be showers, parties, and gifts for them, but Michael and Shawn were not any other couple. It seemed so unfair that because they were a gay couple, they would miss out on all of that. But when Michael called to say that he and Shawn had registered at the wedding department at Bloomingdales, my concerns vanished. I was delighted and struck by my son's boldness. If anyone thought for one minute we were slinking into this, they would have to think again. Shame, so often an uninvited guest in my life, would not be welcome at this event.

The ceremony was planned for the fall at the home of one of Michael's close friends in the Hamptons, on Long Island. It was a beautiful space—just the right setting for an outdoor wedding. Once the place was fixed, Michael and Shawn asked Hedy to perform the ceremony. We were all thrilled when she said yes. No one could create a sacred space like Hedy, and we knew the ceremony would be exceptional. She and her husband Yumi officiated at Howard and Liz's wedding the year before. What a grand event that was, filled with heart, and overflowing with joy.

Finally the date rolled around and a few days before the Sunday ceremony, Syd and I flew to New York to help with the preparations. It had been years since either of us had been up north in the fall, and on the drive out to the Hamptons we were captivated by the scenery. Living in Florida, how I had missed the beauty of fall, always my favorite season. It was thrilling to see the autumn leaves in a glorious profusion of reds, oranges, yellows and greens, coloring the landscape. When we got to our hotel, we checked in, unpacked, and then went exploring. The town was beautiful with a quiet elegance, reminding me of where I had lived as a girl in Philadelphia.

Friday morning, Syd and I went to "ceremony central" our nickname for the home where the festivities would take place, and did some preparations for the *Shabbat* (Sabbath) dinner we would be hosting later that night. Then we headed for the airport to pick up our friends, Louise and Frank. Louise had shared so much of the early painful part of my journey, having her and Frank there was especially meaningful for me. A short time later, Syd's Aunt Helen's plane arrived. She was eighty years old, and had to take two planes to get there, but this was her godson's Commitment Ceremony, and there was no way she would have missed it.

Our next stop was back to ceremony central, to meet Shawn's family for the first time. Under most circumstances, meeting in-laws isn't easy, and these circumstances were, well, certainly unusual. But what we discovered was that in spite of any differences, the love we shared for our children created an instant bond between us. It hadn't even been a year since Shawn's family found out that he was gay. In light of where Syd and I were emotionally after Michael first came out, we were impressed with how loving and accepting they were.

Once other friends and family had arrived, we gathered together in a circle, where I welcomed this special group of kindred spirits, joined by our connection to Michael and Shawn. What a diverse group we were, and hearing how far we all had traveled to be there—both literally and figuratively—created a real sense of community among us. After everyone spoke, we said traditional Friday night prayers, ate dinner, schmoozed and got to know each other. The evening was a special one—wonderfully warm—very *Haimish* (homey). I think we all had a sense that the weekend wasn't only about building new bridges; it was about crossing them as well. One thing we all knew for sure, we weren't in Kansas anymore. It was a perfect beginning for the most extraordinary weekend.

Much to our surprise and dismay, on Saturday morning we woke up in the middle of an unexpected storm, a Nor'easter, something we didn't see coming. Being Floridians, Syd and I were familiar with hurricanes barreling through, often leaving a path of destruction in a matter of hours, but this storm was another story; it didn't want to quit. All that day and night it poured with no signs of stopping and the wind came in strong, unsteady gusts. The Sunday ceremony was planned for outside and we wondered what it would take to move things inside. But since we had no control over the weather, we decided no sense letting it spoil the weekend. We'd figure it out when the time came.

People continued arriving, including friends Michael had known since elementary school days. When his college girlfriend, arrived, she and I had a loving, bittersweet reunion. I'll always have a special place in my heart for her. Married now, she and Michael have remained very dear friends.

On Saturday afternoon, Michael and Shawn arranged for their guests to go wine tasting at a nearby vineyard. The weather wasn't cooperating at all, but we didn't let it dampen our spirits. To get to the winery we had to take two ferries through stormy seas, pouring rain, and gusty winds—quite an adventure. But it was great fun and we all had the best time. Almost everyone went, even Aunt Helen, and after a few glasses of wine we all forgot about the weather.

Later that night, the rain showed no signs of stopping, and seemed to be coming down in bucketfuls when Syd and I made our way to the restaurant for the rehearsal dinner we were hosting for the out of town guests. When Michael's high school girlfriend arrived, she was literally wringing wet. But she didn't care, she wouldn't let anything, not even a Nor'easter, keep her away. The love she brought with her was palpable. Years earlier, when I was so absorbed in my own issues, she and her sister were wonderful friends to Michael. I've always loved them for being there for him during that time he so needed support.

When he was five years old, Michael had been the ring bearer at his aunt's wedding. We found out how much of an impression that made on him when he welcomed everyone, saying that from the time he was five he started thinking about what his wedding would be like—and this was not it! Everyone laughed, especially Syd and me—this wasn't "it" for us either!

I welcomed everyone, acknowledging the stormy conditions outside by saying, "This recreating the human community isn't so easy."

There was a loud drum roll of thunder and a crack of lightning as if to emphasize my words, and I saw agreeing heads bobbing around the room.

"For me this storm is a metaphor for what those of us who support the gay community will have to face in days and probably years to come," I went on. "But, even though mainstream acceptance of gay relationships will most likely be filled with inclement weather such as this, it won't last forever. Eventually the sun will come out!"

I hoped it would be tomorrow. We shared a delightful evening with good food and wonderful company. It was still pouring when we left, but Syd and I only got wet on the outside; inside we felt warm and cozy.

When we got back to our hotel room, I switched on The Weather Channel, hoping Sunday's forecast would be for clear skies, but it was for more of the same: overcast and continued rain. Disappointing news, but I didn't dwell on it. After such a full day, I quickly fell asleep, not waking until seven a.m. to the now familiar sound of falling rain. About an hour later I was making a mental list of what had to be done to move the ceremony inside when I glanced out the window. The rain had finally stopped. Taking a closer look, I saw that the clouds were clearing, and in their place were large patches of blue; minutes later, the sun came peeking out! Miraculously, Sunday turned out to be the most perfectly beautiful, sunny fall day anyone could have wished for. But what a mess it was outside. Surveying the aftermath of the previous day, the backyard of ceremony central looked like, well, like a Nor'easter hit it. Cleaning it up before the ceremony was quite a job.

Soon the house was buzzing with preparations. Then Hedy and Yumi arrived and began preparing for the ceremony; and in short order everything was done. Before the guests began arriving, I took a moment to silently thank the people who had lit my way with light and love and helped bring me to this amazing place and time in my life. It was something I never could even have imagined ten years earlier.

Once all the guests had gathered, Hedy had us share our connection to Michael and Shawn and in minutes all of us felt a bond; we had become a community of well-wishers. As we made our way outside for the ceremony, the weather couldn't have been more delightful. It seemed unimaginable that yesterday there had been such a horrific storm. Before entering the *Chupah*, (a temporary shelter Jewish couples traditionally stand under when saying their vows), Michael and Shawn expressed their heartfelt gratitude to everyone for being a part of such an important day in their lives. Usually rectangular in shape, this brightly colored Chupah was triangular, symbolic of gay pride.

Before they exchanged vows, a piano was brought outside and three male friends, all theater people, performed a hauntingly beautiful love song, "In Whatever Time We Have," from the show *Children of Eden* by Stephen Schwartz. The strains of music exquisitely played filled the air encircling us. The song may have been written for a man and woman, but when it was sung by two men, for two men; it was a perfect expression of love:

> *There are times I've been afraid,*
> *in a world that's so uncertain.*
> *Then I feel your hand in mine,*
> *and there's courage in my heart.*
> *We could live a hundred years,*
> *or the world could end tomorrow.*
> *But we know we'll be together*
> *in whatever time we have.*[5]

As I listened to the words I remembered how, years earlier, I had fervently wished for Michael to be in a heterosexual, even if loveless, marriage. How much simpler my life would have been, I thought at the time. But now I knew this wasn't about my life, it was about Michael's and I felt so thankful that my son had made the choice to live his life authentically.

---

[5] Lines from "In Whatever Time We Have" by Stephen Schwartz from the musical play *Children of Eden*, © 1991 by Grey Dog Music, are reprinted with permission.

When Michael thanked his brother Howard for being such a *Mensch* (righteous person) and for teaching him so much about relationships, tears sprang to my eyes. They had their issues growing up, but over the years they had come to appreciate each other. Then Michael thanked Syd, saying the one person he could always count on to be there for him was his father. Truer words were never spoken. When he thanked me for teaching him about unconditional love, I thought, "how ironic—I was the one who learned that from him!"

A special moment following the blessing and pronouncement was the breaking of two glasses. One glass was broken by Michael, in the traditional Jewish way, the other shattered by Shawn to symbolize breaking the taboo against gay unions. Michael and Shawn shared a kiss and with a hearty *Mazel Tov* (good luck), the ceremony ended.

When the food was being served, Syd and I slipped away from the group for a quiet moment together. We found an out of the way place, there was music playing in the background, and quite unexpectedly, Syd took me in his arms, and we started dancing. The song was: "I'll Always Love You," by Taylor Dayne. The lyrics were a perfect expression of our feelings for one another. No one but the two of us could have known all that we had been through to arrive at this place, fully present, fully conscious, completely in tune and connected to each other. It was an unforgettable moment—a peak experience in our lives.

Throughout the day, I heard things like: "Thank you for showing us how to do this"..."The ceremony had such soul"…"I've never been to anything like it before"… "As a mother I can only imagine what you and your family must have gone through to get to this day"…"What a journey it must have been for you." Truly it had been.

Later, at the hotel, a group of us congregated in Michael and Shawn's room, and had a wonderful time sipping champagne and nibbling on fruit as the guys opened their gifts. The weekend was one of the highlights of my life being there one hundred percent, with my precious husband at my side. If I hadn't chosen to take the journey, I doubt I could have been there at all, and even if I had, it certainly wouldn't have been with this level of consciousness.

It seems to me when two people come together as one, beginning a life together, the defining element isn't whether the event is a wedding between a man and woman, a commitment ceremony with two men, or a union of two women. What gives the occasion meaning, what matters, when all is said and done, is the love they share.

CHAPTER 14

THANKS FOR SHARING

This being human is a guest house.
Every morning is a new arrival.
A joy, a depression, a meanness,
some momentary awareness comes
as an unexpected visitor.
Welcome and entertain them all!
Even if they're a crowd of sorrows
who violently sweep your house
empty of all its furniture,
still, treat each guest honorably.
He may be clearing you out for some new delight.
The dark thought, the shame, the malice,
meet them at the door laughing, and invite them in.
Be grateful for whatever comes,
because each has been sent as a guide from beyond.
(Rumi)

❧

Over the years I've had some interesting interactions with people, some that were uplifting, some far from it. All were growth experiences, though, and in the long run; I grew stronger, and learned more about myself because of them. But what remains most vivid in my mind are both the interactions that tried my patience and those that lightened my spirit. Following are some of the stories that stand out in my memory, beginning with one that was quite unsettling at the time.

Syd and I were hosting a Chanukah party for our *Haverah* (a group of friends who celebrate Jewish holidays together). First to arrive was a young woman and her teenage daughter, who I hadn't met before. Our yearly Chanukah gift exchange was very popular, and it wasn't unusual for people, who weren't part of our group to show up for the party. They told me they heard about the get-together from mutual friends, so I welcomed them and invited them in. They were curious about the Haverah and I was telling them about it when we found ourselves in my kitchen. I noticed the woman looking at the many pictures that covered my refrigerator. She pointed to one of me with Michael, "Is that your son?" She asked.

"Yes," I said proudly, and she commented on how handsome he is.

I thanked her and she asked, "Is he married?"

"No," I answered, "He's not, but he's in a committed relationship." I could have left it at that, but added, "He's gay."

It was no secret. There are pictures of my children all over my home, including ones of Michael and Shawn. But as soon as I heard the woman's response, I realized I made a mistake. Later I wondered, what was I thinking? I didn't know anything about these people or how they felt about gays. But for a moment, in the safety of my home, I didn't think—I just spoke. Not a good idea.

"Oh, what a shame," the woman said, matter-of-factly, assuming, I can only suppose, that I would feel the same way. Up shot my antenna.

"We don't think so," I said unapologetically speaking for Syd and me. But she wasn't hearing what I said, and continued on in the same vein, as though this was nothing more than a casual conversation we were having.

Shaking her head from side to side, she said mindlessly, "It's such a waste, isn't it?"

She seemed completely oblivious to the fact that this was my child she was talking about. I thought of a Woody Allen line, "If God is testing us, couldn't he give us a written?"

I braced myself for what might come next and said, "Well, my husband and I don't feel that way."

The daughter chimed in with a condescending, "Isn't that sweet." Her comment, dripping with sarcasm, sounded anything but sweet to me.

Wondering how to bring this conversation to an end, I said with some finality, "Sweet or not, we're fine with it. Having a gay son isn't a problem for us."

The woman was clearly flustered by my response. Had she ever heard anyone admit to having a gay son before? Probably not, and I'd venture a guess that hearing anyone speak about their gay son with acceptance was not even within her realm of possibility.

Trying to recover, she said patronizingly, "Oh, there's nothing wrong with it. Gays are the same as everyone else."

I was waiting for her to say that some of her best friends were gay, but before she could subject me to that worn-out cliché, thankfully, other guests began arriving. I was relieved to welcome them and be done with such an unpleasant exchange. I put my feelings up on the shelf to deal with later and after everyone left, I retrieved them.

Even though this woman's comments were insensitive and inappropriate, I honestly didn't think she intended to insult me; she was, after all, a guest in my home. She may have even thought she was paying me a compliment along the lines of, "he's so good looking, it's a shame he's unavailable." But what really bothered me was that she spoke with no awareness that she had crossed a line, and had violated polite social norms. I don't even think it occurred to her that she had insulted me. Because in her mind, she was most probably, simply stating a conventional truism.

As I thought of all the things I should have said, could have said, wished I had said, I became irate that this woman felt she had the right to speak to me so crassly in my own home yet. But the anger bubbling up wasn't only toward her; it was toward myself for not having the presence of mind to say more than I did. And that wasn't all. I was outraged at our very homophobic world for painting a shame-filled picture of gays, and then framing it in such utter contempt, that by society's standards, her words were acceptable. Adding fuel to that fire was my knowing that this woman wasn't only speaking for herself; she spoke for a lot of other people who felt the same way. I kept trying to make sense of it and wondered if her attitude was caused by prejudice or ignorance. Maybe a little of both, I decided. What I kept coming back to, though, was this: what kind of a mother would deliberately say such things to another mother, without a moment's hesitation? Could she be that dense?

As I was mulling over this woman's comments—all right, ruminating would be a better word—I was getting angrier by the minute, and feeling very self-righteous about the whole thing. Then, suddenly an image popped into my mind that brought me back to an earlier time. There I was in my mind's eye, describing a good-looking gay man to a friend, and I was using that very expression, "what a waste." Whoa. That put a damper on my self-righteous indignation. Granted, I wasn't speaking about her child, but imagine the irony of hearing those same words echoed back at me now. Along with that realization came a most uncomfortable epiphany. This woman and I weren't so different after all. What was different was our life circumstances. If I didn't have a gay son, just how different would I be from her? Probably not so very. Like her, I might still be blind to my own bigotry, while convinced I was the picture of tolerance and acceptance. It was quite a sobering thought.

This brief episode in front of my refrigerator sure jolted me back to reality. For over a decade I had surrounded myself with loving, open-minded people, and naively I had forgotten that not everyone in the world is as accepting of gay people as my friends. I wondered if I could have said anything to let this mother and daughter know how hurtful and inappropriate their comments were. A line from Kurt Vonnegut came to mind, "So it goes." There was nothing more to be said. They were where they were, stuck in their judgment about gays, like I was not all that long ago. The fact was their comments said a whole lot more about the two of them than they said about my family. Finally I was able to let it go. Maybe my open acceptance of my son gave them pause to think, but whether it did or not, I had no doubt they must have had a lulu of a conversation on the way home.

Then there was the time I told Joan, a casual friend, that Michael was gay. Her response floored me.

She said, "You remember my daughter, Pati, well she thought she was gay too, but after we 'laid down the law' she recanted. Anyway, we don't believe in it."

"Believe in what?" I asked.

"Being gay." She said, "And we let Pati know in no uncertain terms that if she was gay, she wasn't our daughter."

That didn't leave Pati many options. I suppose Joan was expecting me to agree with her. But I said, "I don't feel that way. I think most people are born gay or straight; they don't choose their sexual orientation. And if Pati was born gay then how can it be wrong? Pati just wanted to be accepted for who she is, and to feel okay about expressing her God-given sexuality. I know it's not easy to accept Joan, believe me, I know. But, if she's gay, she's gay. What can you do?"

"Well, what will that get you?" Joan asked rhetorically, not waiting for an answer. "You can be sure nothing good will come from that kind of thinking. Besides now Pati is married and everyone's happy."

Well, maybe not everyone, I couldn't help but think, since I knew gay people who, fearing their family's rejection, spent years in unhappy, loveless marriages. Pati, like many people, couldn't deal with losing her family, so she did what she felt she had to do to keep them—and so did Joan, who chose to ignore the issue and *fix* her daughter instead.

Joan, like a lot of people, needed to believe that things in her life were the way they were "supposed" to be. That kept her stuck in denial, and since she was comfortable with things the way they were, there was no room for change—at least not on her part.

Unlike Joan, much of my journey has been about getting rid of the "suppose to's," and being open to change. Like the time we were visiting Michael and Shawn in New York and the four of us went to Friday night services at the Gay and Lesbian Synagogue in Manhattan. I wasn't sure what to expect, but kept an open mind. It didn't take long before Syd and I felt at ease. It was Fourth of July weekend and when services were over a young lesbian woman visiting from Israel played a keyboard and sang Hebrew songs. We all joined in, and then began doing some Israeli dances together. After the communal dancing was over the music continued, and soon women began dancing with women, and men began dancing with men. Seeing same-sex couples dancing together felt strange to me at first, but after a while the strangeness wore off, and it seemed so natural that Syd and I got up, and we started dancing too. There we were, the only straight couple on the floor, and suddenly it hit me; I was no longer in the usual ninety-some percent of the population, now I was in the six to ten percent part. I have to say it was an unfamiliar feeling.

It opened my eyes to how the people around me on the dance floor must have felt in so many situations as they went about their daily lives. Out in public they couldn't always be themselves; here at least they could. How freeing that must have been for everyone there. As I glanced around the room what I saw was a small moment, filled with possibility of the way it could be, all of us dancing with the partner who fit for us, without fear of judgment from others. At the end of the evening I had a much greater appreciation for how difficult life could be for gay people, even when it came to something as simple as who it was okay to dance with.

Reaching that level of understanding, I wanted to say more and do more to help change people's perceptions about gays. I had the opportunity with a family we met while taking a four-day cruise. At dinner Syd and I were seated with a couple that were, we assumed, with their two grown daughters. An average American family, I thought. It turned out that the man and woman had only recently married and were traveling with her daughter and the daughter's friend, both in their twenties. They were all very congenial and during our dinners together the conversation was lively and interesting. Then one evening in the course of conversation, the woman asked if both of our sons were married.

Well, here it is, I thought. How do I answer that question? I glanced over at Syd and we smiled at one another. I could have just said "yes, both of our sons are married," since in our minds and hearts that's true. But there's a saying, "If you always do what you always did, you'll always get what you always got."

And since I have this thing about putting it out into the universe that being straight or gay is nothing more than someone's sexual orientation, instead I said, "Our younger son is married, and our older son is gay and in a committed relationship."

There was an uncomfortable moment of quiet. Then the daughter, Lynn, asked, "How long was it before you were able to accept that your son was gay?"

"Quite a few years," I said. "It wasn't an overnight thing. It took a lot of work for us to get where we are now."

"How did you find the wherewithal to do it?" She asked.

"It was my child," I said. "I had to find a way to make sense of it."

"I can't get over that you're willing to talk so openly about it," Lynn responded, and then began asking one question after the other. It didn't feel like she was prying; her questions were nonjudgmental, filled with simple curiosity, and she listened thoughtfully to each answer.

It was as though she was weighing each one, until finally she said, "We seem to have something in common." That certainly piqued my interest. "Two years ago my parents divorced after being married for over twenty-five years. It all happened so fast— right after my father came out as a gay man. I was stunned by the whole thing."

Up to this point, while our conversation hadn't been exactly what you'd call typical table chatter, Lynn's comment took it to a whole new level. Now we were getting very real.

I glanced over at Lynn's mother. She said, "You'll pardon me if I stay out of this part of the conversation."

I nodded. Our exchange couldn't have been comfortable for her; we all understood that and respected her boundaries.

"The hardest part for me was I never had any idea that my father was gay until the divorce." Lynn said. "I couldn't understand why he would do this to us; why he felt the need to come out, and why now. I was devastated by it, and hated him for tearing our family apart. But now I've come to see that my father spent his whole life living this carefully constructed lie, because he felt he had no alternative. He was terrified that if he were honest about himself, he'd lose his family. But after he met his partner, my father said he could not live the lie one more day. I know this will sound strange, but my father and I are closer now than we ever were before."

"It doesn't sound strange at all," I answered. "Have you ever heard the saying, 'we're only as sick as our secrets'? Now that this one is out in the open, there are no walls between you."

"It's such a relief," Lynn said. "My father and his partner just had a commitment ceremony. I can't even begin to describe it. I only hope when I get married my wedding will be as meaningful."

"Your father is very courageous to reclaim his life, in spite of all he had to lose." Syd commented.

"The divorce was an awful mess. But, in spite of everything, I love my father. He was always the most wonderful dad, and is now more than ever."

As we were leaving the table Lynn and I shared a hug. I said, "Your willingness to accept your dad isn't only a gift to him, it's a gift to yourself."

"It's true. Most people wouldn't understand that," Lynn said. "Thank you, thank you for understanding."

Her mother took me aside and said, "I want to thank you for giving Lynn the opportunity to talk about this in such a positive way. It's not the kind of thing that gets talked about so openly, and I see how much it meant to her."

While our conversation with this family wasn't life-changing for any of us, I think it made a difference to Lynn. I know it made a difference to me. So often what lurks in the dark, whether real or imagined, remains in the shadows, until someone sheds light, even if just a little, on what otherwise can be a taboo subject.

So what is an average American family, anyway? And is there really such a thing? Like many of us, I grew up being taught that a family was a group consisting of two parents and their children, living together as a unit. That's one definition. But it seems that in the twenty-first century, definitions of family are as varied as families are themselves. In today's world, for me there's a better description: family is the place where people love and accept one another the way they are, unconditionally; where members support each other, and where it's safe for everyone just to be themselves. That may not always be the way it is in our family of origin, but it can be in our family of choice. Over the years, certainly since the time Michael first came out, our culture has become more open-minded and accepting, and in time I believe society's definition of family will change and evolve too, one family at a time. That already seems to be happening. Results of a recent poll showed that over seventy per cent of the U.S. population knew someone gay and many were accepting of gay unions. It seems being gay is less of an anomaly, and that the shroud of shame and mystery surrounding it for so many years is finally lifting.

After Syd and I got back from our trip, we gave our conversation with Lynn some thought, and decided to branch out and see if we could find a way to make a difference in our community. By this time we had been going to PFLAG meetings for over ten years. With only a few exceptions (that were few and far between), we were pretty much the only Jewish parents who came to the meetings. When someone asked us about it, Syd said, "Not to worry, we have plenty of Catholics to provide the guilt." That was true enough. But we wondered how to begin breaking down the barriers that kept Jewish parents, not only from coming to PFLAG meetings, but from coming out at all. We went to speak with two local Rabbis both known for their open and liberal views (we didn't want to hear about Leviticus), to see if they had any ideas or advice on how we could go about it. Though we met with each of them separately, I can't say that we were surprised when we got pretty much the same response. Both Rabbis were gay friendly, both had performed commitment ceremonies for gay couples, and both had counseled gay and lesbian members of their congregations. But in all their years in the Rabbinate, no parent ever came to see either of them for counseling because they had a gay child, or ever even mentioned it, for that matter. It was clear we were in for an uphill battle. The Rabbis said they'd like to help but weren't sure how. They wished us good luck. We would need it.

Since many cities offered groups and programs for their gay populations, Syd and I thought, why not ours? Not that we didn't know why not. We weren't living in a vacuum. Orlando wasn't exactly on the cutting edge of such things, but it was where we lived. So our next step was to make an appointment with the programming director of the Orlando JCC (Jewish Community Center)

Whether Orlando was ready to come out of the closet remained to be seen, but we were ready, and it was time. Though there was no doubt in my mind that after our meeting at the JCC, news of Michael being gay would spread faster than feathers on a windy day, which of course it did. But I was way past caring about that.

We arrived at the JCC and after exchanging small talk and pleasantries, the program director looked expectantly, waiting to hear what brought us there. I plunged right in, "Almost every religious denomination in Central Florida is doing something for their gay and lesbian population," I said. "But not us. There are no programs or groups of any kind being offered to gays by the Jewish community."

"Do you think Orlando has a gay and lesbian Jewish population?" She asked.

"Yes," I said, "about six to ten percent of Jewish parents have a gay or lesbian child, the same as the rest of the population."

"But I'm not aware of any gay people in our community," she commented.

"They're out there," I responded, "but they're closeted. What we're hoping is that the JCC will open that closet by offering a support group for parents with gay children."

"It sounds like a good idea," she said, trying to be supportive. "But do you really think anyone would come to that kind of group?"

"I understand your concern," I said, "and truthfully, it's not likely. But even if that's the case, won't just offering the group show support for our gay community?"

"I guess that's true," the program director said. "But who would facilitate the group? "

"We'll do it, " we said, "because our son Michael is gay, and we think it's time to open that door. Don't you?"

So a few weeks later, out went a bulletin to most of the Jewish community, announcing upcoming programs that included a listing of our support group for parents with gay children. We waited for the calls to come pouring in (just kidding). The only calls I got were from friends wishing us luck and congratulations for making such a bold move. We didn't give up—yet. For the next year the JCC advertised the group—all told we got three calls. That was it. It wasn't much. The lack of participation only validated how much shame and fear came with the territory. Sure, it would have been great to throw open the door of our very closeted Jewish community, but keeping it real, we were happy that at least we got to put a key in the door. And who knows, maybe the most important thing we did was break a taboo, by publicly announcing to the Jewish community, that there actually are Jewish parents with a gay child who don't think it's a *shunda*.

Not having the group was a disappointment, but we were making progress, maybe not in the Jewish community, but in the Christian one. About two years later we were contacted by the chaplain of a local Presbyterian church, asking us if we would be open to leading a support group for a few of their members who had gay children. We jumped at the chance.

The group was made up of seven people who, as it turned out; all knew each other, some for twenty years. It was quite a shock for them to discover that each of them had a gay child, and not one had a clue about the other. That certainly broke the ice and made for an interesting beginning to the six-week group. The rest of the evening they shared how and when they heard the news, and how they coped with it.

One of the women chastised herself; "I can't believe that as a mother I didn't know. Honestly it never entered my mind that Brian could be gay. When he told me I was shocked. I thought he just hadn't met the right girl yet—even though he was thirty-five and never brought a girl home to meet me. It broke my heart that he lived with this for so long and didn't feel he could come to me."

A couple with a lesbian daughter said, "We suspected Meg was gay for a long time. There were signs since she was a teenager. During high school, she dated a little, but after her graduation we noticed the boys didn't come around anymore, and there always seemed to be talk about this girl or that. We wanted to ask, but didn't know how to bring it up. It's not like there's a how-to book on the right way to do it. And what if we were wrong? That would have been a big muddle, so we never said anything. When she broke the news, we were relieved to have it out in the open."

Not everyone in the group was so accepting, but they were all in agreement that they had a lot to learn about homosexuality. They knew their understanding of it was limited, and they were willing to stretch. One of the biggest concerns for everyone was what to do about other people's reactions, especially those of family members and members of their church, some who were deeply polarized about gays. In a later group, we brainstormed questions that people might ask, and ways to respond to negative comments that might come.

From our first meeting, Syd and I were impressed not only with the depth that people shared, but in the way they listened—with loving attention and genuine caring. Discovering that they weren't the only ones at their church with a gay child, that people they knew and respected had a gay child too, made it easier for them to come out of their isolation. The proverbial cat was finally out of the bag, and everyone felt safe enough to share their feelings, strengthen old bonds, and develop a caring network of understanding friends.

The last night of the group we talked about where each of us wanted to be in five years, and what we needed to do to get there. The consensus seemed to be: to leave their shame behind and build a solid bridge back to their children.

When the group ended we all left knowing that we were connected through a club, which, maybe we wouldn't have joined voluntarily, but one we were members of all the same. On our way home I commented to Syd that even though we were from a different religious tradition, how alike their journey was to ours, as it seems to be for so many parents of gay children, regardless of their religion or lack of it.

Encouraged by our support group, I wanted to keep up the momentum in whatever way I could, even if in small ways. I had that chance when Syd and I were on a trip to North Carolina. In just about every town we drove through there was a restaurant belonging to a chain we never frequented. In fact, we made it a point, sometimes driving miles out of our way, not to eat there, because of their well-known discriminatory practices against gays. But, like the rest of the country, even this chain had become more accepting and recently added sexual orientation to their nondiscrimination policy. So, we decided if they could change their policy, so could we. We stopped there for dinner. After our meal, as we were leaving, the hostess asked, "How was everything?"

"Good," I said. "This is our first time eating here, and we enjoyed it."

"It is?" She asked, looking up somewhat surprised.

"It is," I repeated. "The reason we've never come here before was because of your discrimination policy toward gays and lesbians." An uncomfortable look crossed her face. "But since you've changed your policy, we thought we'd give it a try."

The hostess paused for a long moment, busying herself at the cash register. "Well, I hope you'll come back," she said.

"We will," I responded. "And we'd like to thank you for being more tolerant."

It was just a small thing, but on the way to the car, I was glad I spoke up. I figured the restaurant probably got a whole lot more negative feedback about their policy changes than positive, and it was important to validate their more inclusive policy toward gays.

It was encouraging to know that a large restaurant chain was willing to make such a considerable change. Unfortunately there are some people who are not so inclined; their opinions are carved in stone—no sense trying to change their minds. I learned that first hand when Natalie, a woman I knew asked me, "Why do you think Michael is gay?"

I said I didn't know and she said, "Well, I'll tell you what I think. Everyone knows children are gay because they have a domineering mother. It's common knowledge."

Up went my antenna. Better be careful, I thought to myself. I was being told, and in no uncertain terms, that the reason my son was gay was because of me. It was my fault. I stifled an urge to lash out—what good would that do?—instead I took a deep breath.

Then, with as much patience as I could muster, I said, "The domineering mother and passive father theory is obsolete; that kind of thinking went the way of phonographs and 78 rpm records. I believe most people are born gay or straight, and I'm not alone in that belief."

Natalie was unconvinced. "I don't believe that—not for one minute."

Then, realizing I suppose, that she had gone too far, she said, "Well, maybe that's not the way it is in your family, but I know someone else who's very domineering, and I'm sure that's why her child is gay."

Was God testing me again? Apparently so. No written exam here. I could only imagine the grief this conversation could have caused me if it had taken place at the beginning of my journey when, like most mothers, I did believe that old wives' tale. No doubt it would have crushed me. Thankfully, now I was in a very different place. And anyway, anyone who knows me knows that I was so not a domineering mother, but even if I had been, that's not why Michael was gay. Although that old label is one that still gets pinned on moms.

I was done with this conversation. It had no way to go but further downhill, so I considered the source and changed the subject. Like the woman at my

Chanukah party, Natalie was completely unaware that her words were like arrows. It was a good thing I was able to deflect them. What was truly ironic about the whole thing was that I knew Natalie's mother and she was one of the most domineering women on the planet. If I could go back (don't we all want to do that sometimes?) and have that conversation today, what I'd say is, "Considering the mother you had, Natalie, with that kind of logic why aren't you gay?"

What I learned from that experience is that if someone knows what they know, and they aren't willing to consider another point of view, it's best not to waste your time or energy on them. It's likely they have a very different agenda than yours, and they're not likely to change anytime soon.

For most of us change doesn't come easy, but if we want to let go of old ways of doing things, I've found it's usually best to embrace it. Since we now have a Christian son-in-law, Syd and I have become more open and inclusive when it comes to celebrating our traditions. One of my fondest memories is one December weekend we spent with Michael and Shawn during Chanukah and Christmas in the Catskill Mountains. Being full-fledged Floridians, Syd and I hadn't seen snow in years and we weren't prepared for it, but the guys brought sweaters and coats, even boots, to keep us warm. And honestly, to be sitting in front of a warm fire, sipping hot chocolate, with a blanket of snow all around us was lovely for a change.

Shawn was busy studying, so he sent the three of us out to buy a Christmas tree, a first for me. Checking out the trees, Michael commented, "Here we are, three Jews buying a Christmas tree. Did you ever think you'd ever be doing this, mom?"

No I didn't, and the irony of it didn't escape us.

Later that day, Syd and I made potato *latkas* (pancakes), a traditional food for Chanukah, and Michael lit the Chanukah Menorah (candles). After dinner we decorated pinecones with glitter, made ornaments, and helped trim the tree. It was anything but a traditional first night of Chanukah, but it was an honoring of our traditions, Shawn's and ours. The paradox was that by taking part in each other's rituals, we each felt more connected to our own heritage and to each other.

Little did Syd and I know it but big changes were on the horizon for us. Soon we'd be sharing our thoughts with thousands of people in Orlando.

Along with a group from PFLAG, Syd and I went to speak to Tom Dyer, publisher of *Watermark*, the bi-monthly gay newspaper in Central Florida. Our chapter had an idea about a monthly column for *Watermark*, written by different PFLAG parents, who would tell their coming-out stories, and we wanted to run it by Tom. He thought about it for a minute and said he didn't think it would work, but asked, what about having the same two parents write a column each month? As far as he knew there were no other gay publications that had a column written by parents. Then he turned to Syd and me, and asked, "What do the two of you think about that?"

when we said we thought it was a good idea, Tom asked if we'd like to write the column. It was an unexpected, but intriguing idea. We told him we needed some time to think about it; both of us already had full schedules, and writing a monthly column would take a big commitment of time. We talked about it on the way home and before we reached our front door, decided it was a great opportunity; let's do it.

Two months later, our first article was published in a column we went on to write for three years, "A Parent's Perspective." It gave us the chance to add our voices publicly to the cause of gay acceptance, and to validate the gay sons and lesbian daughters in our community who had no one to support or speak for them. It's one of the things I'm proudest of. Mainly the articles were stories of our journey, like the ones in this chapter, and the feedback we got from the local community made it all worthwhile.

A postscript: Interestingly, a few months before our meeting with Tom, Syd and I were at a New Year's retreat with a group of friends where we talked about our goals for the coming year. One of my goals was to have something of mine published and to be paid for it. Little did I know just months later, that would happen, when to my surprise a check from *The Watermark* arrived in the mail! It was so out of the blue. I had no idea we'd be paid for our columns, and I was delighted. Funny how things work out: in my mind it was my children's book I saw being published. Writing for *The Watermark* wasn't even on my radar screen. So, it turned out I did achieve my goal—just not in the way I expected.

How unpredictable life is, and how full of lessons. One of those lessons was, that when an exciting and challenging opportunity comes along, even if it's a stretch, welcome it. It just might be the universe offering some new possibility.

CHAPTER 15

EFFECTS OF HOMOPHOBIA

You've got to be taught to hate and fear,
You've got to be taught from year to year,
It's got to be drummed in your dear little ear.
You've got to be carefully taught!

You've got to be taught to be afraid
Of people whose eyes are oddly made,
And people whose skin is a different shade,
You've got to be carefully taught.

You've got to be taught before it's too late,
Before you are six or seven or eight,
To hate all the people your relatives hate,
You've got to be carefully taught!
You've got to be carefully taught![6]
(from the musical South Pacific by Richard
Rodgers and Oscar Hammerstein II)

ᕲᕽ

---

[6] "You've Got to be Carefully Taught" by Richard Rodgers and Oscar Hammerstein II. Copyright © 1949 by Richard Rodgers and Oscar Hammerstein II. Copyright Renewed. WILLIAM-SON MUSIC owner of publication and allied rights throughout the World. International Copyright Secured. All Rights Reserved. Used by Permission.

And so we were, carefully taught during childhood when the seeds of prejudice are sown, and then harvested, as we grow older. Like most people, I saw myself as open-minded and tolerant, and I was—to a point. But growing up I heard a lot of prejudiced messages, some inadvertently from family members, teachers, and other respected adults. The simple truth is nearly all of us have been brought up in a society that's homophobic. And whether we see it or not, there are countless ways all of us have internalized the messages we received from the world around us—both consciously and unconsciously. Even the most open-minded of us, though we may not be aware of it, are likely to be holding onto some stereotypes.

It wasn't until Syd and I went to *The Experience* that I realized the depth of my own prejudice, particularly when it came to homophobia. Oh, there had been glimpses of it, sure, but at *The Experience* was when I really saw it, up close and personal. I have to admit; it was hard for me to think of myself as homophobic, especially when I had come so far from where I started. But, like it or not, that weekend I realized I wasn't done yet. So to broaden my perspective, I began asking gay people I knew about their coming-out experience. I asked questions like: when did you first know you were gay, how did you know, and what was that discovery like for you. What a learning that was!

Over the years I must have heard hundreds of coming-out stories—from friends and clients, each was unique, but there was one common thread connecting them. Even though some people were too young to understand it, or even have language to express it, everyone knew, when they were quite young, that somehow they were different—in a way that was expressly unacceptable. And as kids are apt to do, they made the assumption there must be something wrong with *them*. Some excelled in school and other areas to compensate, others barely got by. But either way, unconsciously what they all learned, was that if they wanted to fit in and be accepted by their families and the people around them, they would have to put their questions aside and conceal a part of themselves.

Most of the people I spoke to came out in their late teens to early thirties, but their ages ranged from as young as five to as old as seventy-five. Two of the stories I heard that were especially touching were from men on either side of the age span, from youngest to oldest.

Walter, the older man, didn't come out until after his wife had died when he was seventy-five; they had been married for over fifty years. After her death, Walter finally felt the freedom to come out and live his life as the gay man he was. So he wrote each of his children a carefully worded letter, explaining that he had been devoted to their mother during their marriage, but now that she was gone he wanted to live whatever years were left to him, for himself. He told them that he kept his sexual orientation hidden from them for all these years because he felt sure they would reject him if they found out. He knew this revelation wouldn't be easy for them, but he hoped they would understand. Anxiously Walter waited, not knowing if or when he would hear from either of his children. Some weeks later they called, concerned and filled with questions. With time, they got over their disbelief, and when I heard the story, they were, if not accepting, at least staying in touch and keeping the lines of communication open. Now, Walter is living out his elder years active in the gay community with his gay partner. When I heard Walter's story I imagined what it must have been like for him, to grow up in a world that made him feel something as natural as his sexual orientation was sinful. How much regret and shame he must have carried to live his life—seventy-five years of it, living a lie to protect himself.

But the times were very different when Walter was growing up in the 1930s. Most gay people's lives were shrouded in secrecy then, and the handful of people who were openly out, were considered the dregs of "polite" society. Back in the day when Walter was in the army, it was during a time no one even thought of asking, and clearly no one thought of telling, unless they placed little value on their lives. After living through such blatantly homophobic times, I could understand why Walter remained closeted for so many years, but that didn't make it any less heartbreaking. When I heard the following story at a therapy conference, I couldn't help but think of Walter's situation.

A baby elephant, living in captivity, was tied to a tree at night with a strong chain. Instinctively it tried to break free, but being just a baby, it didn't have the strength. Still, it kept trying to free itself, but failed each time, and eventually gave up. When it became an adult, and could easily have broken free by uprooting the tree or breaking the chain, this huge, powerful elephant, weighing several tons no longer made an effort to escape. Even when tied to a twig, it didn't try to free itself, it simply accepted its fate. The elephant had limited its present abilities by limitations of the past. It's a concept called "learned helplessness," first researched by the psychologist Hans Selye. In light of the elephant story, it has also been called "elephant syndrome." It's been said an elephant never forgets—and sometimes neither do people.

The other story that I found so poignant was from Nick, a sixty-year-old man who knew something wasn't right when he was only five years old. His sister brought her boyfriend home to meet the family, and he got a crush on the boyfriend. From the age of five Nick lived in fear of anyone discovering his secret. What were the messages he got at the age of five that told him there was something very wrong, not only with what he was feeling, but also with who he was? The truth is there was nothing wrong with him, but there was something very wrong with a society that would give such messages to a little boy. With the exception of his sister, Nick hid his sexual orientation from his family, and from most of his friends, and as far as I know he still remains in the closet.

Then there was Keith's story. Keith, a thirty-year old client I was seeing in therapy, told me by the time he was twelve he knew he'd better act straight, talk straight, and be straight if he wanted to keep his family's love. Like so many other gay teens, Keith stuffed his feelings and got so good at hiding them; he was no longer sure who he was. It took years before he faced the truth about his sexual orientation and was able to come out first to himself, and later to his family. Growing up Keith walked a tightrope between fulfilling his family's expectations of who they thought he should be, and who he actually was. His options were limited as a teen, so he did what he needed to do to survive, and learned to play the role he had to, but in the process he lost himself.

It isn't only gay teens that cope with these kinds of feelings. Straight teens may have similar feelings of not fitting in, or doubts about who they are. But added to the normal angst of adolescence, gay teens are facing atypical anxiety and confusion, as they try to come to grips with their sexual orientation. That doesn't make for an easy transition, not in the homophobic world we live in.

Most of us have been socialized to believe that what's "normal" is being straight and that sexually we're all pretty much the same. But that one-size-fits-all theory doesn't work—not when it comes to sexuality. How could it, when we're all so unique? After extensive research Alfred Kinsey, famous for his groundbreaking work on human sexuality, *Sexual Behavior in the Human Male*, concluded that people do not fit into neat and exclusive heterosexual and homosexual categories. Kinsey developed a scale representing the continuum of human sexuality. Genetically, it's been said; we are ninety-nine percent alike—ah but, that other one percent. That's what makes us who we are.

The Heterosexual/Homosexual Rating Scale[7]

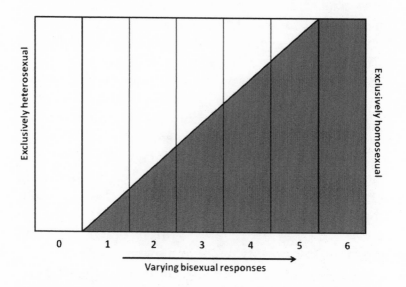

0- Exclusively heterosexual with no homosexual
1- Predominantly heterosexual, only incidentally homosexual
2- Predominantly heterosexual, but more than incidentally homosexual
3- Equally heterosexual and homosexual
4- Predominantly homosexual, but more than incidentally heterosexual
5- Predominantly homosexual, only incidentally heterosexual
6- Exclusively homosexual

---

[7] From *Sexual Behavior in the Human Male* by Alfred C. Kinsey, Wardell B. Pomeroy, and Clyde E. Martin (Philadelphia: W. B. Saunders Co., 1948). Copyright © The Kinsey Institute. Reproduced by permission of The Kinsey Institute for Research in Sex, Gender, and Reproduction, Inc.

Not long ago I counseled a gay man named Matt who was from a strong Christian background. He wasn't able to accept himself, or his sexual orientation, and did everything in his power to "become" straight. Homosexuality went against everything he had ever been taught by his family and by his church. Being gay was unimaginable to him. Matt came to see me after an unsuccessful stint at an "ex-gay" ministry that claimed he could "cure" himself of his homosexuality through redemptive prayer if he had the desire and the will to change. Listening to Matt tell this highly improbable story, I wondered if their theory could also be applied to straight people too. Could they also "cure" straight people with the desire to become gay in the same way? With all their promises, what this "ex-gay" ministry offered Matt was acceptance—albeit conditional, as long as he complied with the behavior and beliefs that they deemed appropriate. In other words: we'll accept you, as long as you declare that you're straight and live as a straight man. But what kind of acceptance is that? What I know from my conversations with gay people is that those who are drawn into groups like this most often have difficulty reconciling their sexual orientation with parental rejection, religious beliefs, and society's disapproval. So to fit in, they suppress their natural inclination. But in spite of reprogramming, abstaining from sex, and/or being placed in heterosexual marriages, people in these ex-gay ministries are set up to fail and dismally at that, leaving them feeling far worse about themselves than they did before. I equate going to an "ex-gay" ministry to dyeing my hair red. People seeing me would most probably assume I was a redhead. But am I? On the surface it would certainly seem so, but in reality the red only lasts until my hair begins growing out, then it returns to my natural color. No matter how much I want to be a redhead or how hard I try to be one, it's just not going to happen, not permanently.

We live in a world where we can easily whiten our teeth, change the color of our hair, and with contact lenses, even the color of our eyes. To keep us looking younger there's plastic surgery—and presto, change-o—a smaller nose—a more chiseled chin—firmer, shapelier breasts. But no matter how many external changes we make, the one thing we can't alter is our fundamental nature, and that's what these "ex-gay" ministries try to do. The reality is if someone is gay, he or she is gay. And no matter how hard you try, you can't change a bird into a fish because you don't like the song it sings. You might teach a bird to swim, but eventually it will fly; that's what birds do. To purposely try to change someone who's gay into someone who's straight by attempting to change his or her natural sexual orientation is, I believe, not only psychologically damaging, it's downright Orwellian. For what purpose is this done to make gay people "straighter" and therefore more acceptable to mainstream society? These "ex-gay" programs persist, though the American Psychiatric Association, the American Psychological Association, and virtually the entire mental health profession have denounced them.

Because homosexuality is such an anomaly to so many people, there's a widely held, but misguided, belief that being gay is a choice—and I was one of the people who held that belief not so long ago. When I read the book, *Is It a Choice?,* written by Eric Marcus, something he said remained percolating in the back of my mind, and while I was writing this it re-surfaced: "We don't choose the person we're sexually attracted to; those feelings come to light as we grow up, whether we're gay, straight or bi." It wasn't an earth-shattering idea, but I hadn't looked at it in that way before, and it made sense to me. There are theories about it, but does anyone really know why we're sexually attracted to one person and not another? So when I thought about attraction simply happening, and that as we mature we become aware of it, that got me thinking about my own sexual orientation—my first crush on a boy in the second grade, and all the other crushes I had growing up. Being in the "normal" majority, it wasn't something I had ever given much thought to, but when I did, it wasn't like I could remember ever making a choice to be straight—I just was—and have been all my life. So if I hadn't chosen my sexual orientation, why did I believe that Michael had?

When you think about it, does it really make sense that a person would choose to be gay if it wasn't their natural preference? I mean, why would someone consciously choose a life where they would be treated like a second-class citizen, not given the right to marry, might lose the love and support of their family, even be ostracized from their religion? That didn't make sense. So, could it be that being gay isn't so much about making a choice, but that the choice is about whether or not to express one's own God-given sexuality?

Sometimes trying to sort it all out can be tricky, though, because there are always exceptions; life as we know is filled with a ton of contradictions. And since we are dealing with human nature that makes the whole choice thing complicated. An instance: Maddy, a straight friend was sexually and emotionally abused by her grandfather for much of her childhood. As soon as she was able, she took off, wanting to get as far away from her grandfather and from her past as she could. But remnants of the abuse were not so easily forgotten and she spent many years in therapy coming to terms with it. Even though Maddy wasn't a lesbian, during those years she lived as one, it was where she felt safe. When she finally met a man she trusted, whose love allowed her to feel safe, she was able to let down her guard and let nature take its course; she's been married now for over twenty years. All of us have been affected by our childhood experiences in ways that aren't always easily explained or understood.

When I was seeing Pete Fischer for therapy, I asked him why he thought so many people were intolerant and sometimes completely irrational when it came to homosexuality. His answer took me by surprise. "More people than you would imagine are very Victorian when it comes to sex. They're uptight, puritanical, and embarrassed even with straight sex, but gay sex? The very thought of it sends them running for the hills."

That, of course, was the bottom line, and was something that I hadn't even considered. Now that I'm a therapist, I've learned how true that is.

A great paradox is that the Bible, or should I say some people's interpretation of the Bible, is often what perpetuates homophobia. So many people quote and misquote Bible passages to support their personal beliefs about the "evils" of homosexuality. They are what Peter Gomes, author of *The Good Book*, calls "selective literalists," picking and choosing passages that suit their agenda. Some portions of the Bible that have gone by the wayside are those that support slavery—we don't hear those much anymore. Thankfully we've come a long way from those days. And what about the passages that call for the death of adulterers, or brides who aren't virgins? Just imagine if people were advocating those passages. A scary thought in today's world don't you think? And with current divorce rates in our country at around fifty percent, it would seem that at least half of the population simply chooses to ignore the Bible's condemnation of divorce. So why is it that people still point to the quotes about the "evils" of homosexuality, when the Bible offers so many more reasons to oppose homophobia than it does homosexuality?

I think a lot of it has to do with superstition and people's fear of anything or anyone too different from them. My mother used to tell that when she was growing up, whenever she tried to use her left hand someone slapped it. To protect herself, she learned to use her right hand, though it was never her natural preference. That was over eighty years ago, when being left-handed was considered a sin by a lot of people—an archaic notion now. But there are people in today's world who believe homosexuality is a sin; much in the same way as people a century ago believed being left-handed was a sin. Out of such superstition, prejudice is born.

There are many ways prejudice takes hold; one could be compared to marinating a chicken. If you pour soy sauce over a chicken and let it sit in the marinade for, say, an hour, the chicken will absorb the pungent, flavorful taste of the sauce, whether it wants to or not. Like that chicken, most of us grew up soaking in a marinade of one kind of prejudice or another and, unbeknownst to us, it became a part of who we are.

Actor Mel Gibson's behavior demonstrated how this plays out when a police officer pulled him over for a traffic violation in 2006 and arrested him for driving under the influence. While in custody, Gibson made widely quoted anti-Semitic remarks. It was quite shocking at the time, but later I learned this wasn't the first time Gibson's prejudice emerged. A few years before this incident, he made appallingly homophobic remarks about gay men and then refused to apologize, saying, "I don't think there's an apology necessary, and I'm certainly not giving one... if someone wants my opinion, I'll give it. What am I supposed to do, lie to them?" But after Gibson's irrational outburst, blaming the Jews for all the wars in the world, he did express regret, saying, "... Please know from my heart that I am not an anti-Semite. I am not a bigot. Hatred of any kind goes against my faith."

Intellectually, that may be what Gibson believed, but under the façade he presents, I saw a very different picture. And what it looked like to me was someone who had been soaking in a toxic marinade of prejudice for a really long time. Like other bigoted people, Gibson didn't know how deep his feelings went—all the way down to the bone. As far as I was concerned, Gibson's homophobic and anti-Semitic remarks were a double whammy, offending me both as a Jew and as a mother of a gay son.

Homophobia is insidious. It begins with a seed of fear planted in fertile ground. When it's fertilized with ignorance, and watered with narrow-mindedness, the crop likely to sprout is irrational hatred.

We only need to remember the tragic killings of Matthew Shepard, Ryan Skipper, and Sean Kennedy—killed for no other reason than they were gay—to know the reality of this truth. In a vicious attack, twenty-one year old Matthew was robbed, brutally beaten, tortured, tied to a fence in a remote, rural area, near Laramie, Wyoming and left to die. Matthew's injuries were fatal. He remained in a coma for five days and never regained consciousness.

I met Ryan Skipper's stepfather (and later his mother) at a PFLAG conference where I heard the story of Ryan's vile murder. Twenty-five year old Ryan had been beaten, stabbed twenty times and had his throat slit by his assailants who left his body by the side of a road in Wahneta, a small town outside Winter Haven, Florida. The accused killers allegedly drove Ryan's blood-soaked car around the county and bragged of killing him.

At that same conference I met Sean Kennedy's mother, Elke, and heard the story of her twenty-year-old son Sean's senseless death. A boy in a parked car asked Sean for a cigarette. Sean gave him one and was walking away when another boy, sitting in the back seat of the car, got out, approached Sean and called him a faggot. Then he punched Sean in the face with such force that he shattered Sean's cheekbones and separated his brain from his brainstem. His injuries were so severe his mother was told he would not survive. He did not. The last word he heard before he died was "faggot." His accused assailant left the scene, then called a friend who knew Sean and left this message on her cell phone: "You tell your faggot friend that when he wakes up he owes me $500 for my broken hand."

Because Sean's attack took place in South Carolina, where they have no hate crime legislation, his assailant was charged with involuntary manslaughter. His sentence was reduced to fifteen months.

Hate crimes like these are increasing. I can't help but feel outraged that our society is so complacent and apathetic about these brutal crimes. How can we as a society allow this kind of violence to continue? How can we excuse it? What of Sean, Ryan, and Matthew's families, of all the thousands of families who have lost children to hate crimes? How are they to pick up the broken pieces of their lives, knowing that so little is being done to stop this kind of violence from continuing?

Homosexuality is not the problem in our world today. The problem is homophobia. And it's not a gay problem. It's society's problem. We all were carefully taught to fear what was too different, to stick to our own kind. But here we are in the twenty-first century; it's a whole new millennium.

Naturalist John Muir said, "When one tugs at a single thing in nature—he finds it attached to the rest of the world." We're all in this together. What affects one of us, affects all of us. Isn't it time to re-educate ourselves and leave behind the prejudice we've carried around for too many generations? Homophobia not only hurts gay people, it hurts the rest of us as well.

CHAPTER 16

WHAT I KNOW NOW THAT I DIDN'T KNOW I KNEW

We do not receive wisdom,
we must discover it for ourselves,
after a journey through the wilderness,
which no one else can make for us,
which no one can spare us,
for our wisdom is the point of view
from which we come at last to regard the world.
(Marcel Proust)

୍ଚ

Realizing that I didn't come from an "Ozzie and Harriet family" (the quintessential 'perfect' TV family of the 1950's and 60's) was stunning for me. Equally stunning was realizing that I wasn't alone—nobody did—not even Ozzie and Harriet. I made that discovery at the most unlikely time while I was in therapy with Hedy. We had a session early one morning, and that evening Syd and I went to the movies to see *The Untouchables*. Something Hedy and I talked about must have been the catalyst, what it was I don't remember. But there I was sitting in a darkened movie theater, munching on popcorn, watching the scene where Robert De Niro playing Al Capone was just about to beat someone's brains out with a baseball bat, when out of nowhere the fog of denial that had surrounded me for over forty years, simply melted away, and a very different scene was playing in my head. In my mind's eye this was the scene I saw:

After our honeymoon, Syd and I were on our way to Florida to begin our married life together when we made a stop in Philadelphia to see my parents. I had just gone through a bout with food poisoning so I wasn't feeling very well, and was having doubts about moving so far away from my family. Even though from the first day I met Syd, being married to him was all I ever wanted, suddenly I didn't know if at twenty, I was ready to be "Sadie, Sadie, married lady." What I needed was a little reassurance. As usual, it came from my father, who reminded me why I married Syd in the first place. But my mother pooh-poohed my feelings and sent me dismissively on my way.

"You have a husband to take care of you now," she said coldly, letting me know that her obligation was over. It didn't seem to matter that I was frightened and sick; she brushed my feelings aside and could hardly wait to get me out of the house and on my way. I was married off; her job was done. Period.

It wasn't the worst thing that ever happened in my life, but for some reason that was the thing that did it—and just like that—my idealized image of how things were when I was growing up—simply vanished. All at once I was seeing parts of my childhood that I never saw before. With each gunshot in the movie, another memory popped into my mind—

like that awful time at the dentist, when I needed my mother to be there for me but instead felt totally abandoned by her.

Then I had the realization of what role I played in our family, and how well I learned to play it. I was my mother's caretaker, confidant—her island of calm. As long as I was the proverbial "good girl," and did what was expected of me, I was safe, but cross my mother, and out I went sometimes literally, sometimes figuratively. I saw how her manipulation kept me in tow, and how hard I tried to please her in return for any scrap of attention. Staying in her good graces had been paramount for me since I was a child. Thirty minutes earlier, I didn't have a clue, but now there came this knowing that growing up, I had an underlying fear that if I wasn't good enough, I could be replaced in my mother's heart, as easily as exchanging one photograph for another in a picture frame. It was simply stunning for me to see the way it actually was—and all this drama playing out to the backdrop of *The Untouchables*. I sat there longing for the movie to end. When finally it did, and we were safely in the car, I broke down sobbing so—I could hardly catch my breath.

Up until that time, I thought my mother could do no wrong. In an instant, that changed. Underneath the sadness of this discovery was a surge of anger, which would remain with me for many years. It seemed to grow, like yeast dough. I kept punching it down, but it continued rising. I tried journaling, hitting my pillow, screaming in my car, but I couldn't seem to get over it. I read books on forgiveness, went to workshops, and tried meditation, but found that letting go was a whole lot easier in concept, than when it came to actually doing it. Still I kept at it, more for my own sanity, than for anything else. But it felt never-ending—with always another layer of stuff to work through.

One day I was on a major rant about something that happened years earlier, not with my mother, but interestingly, with someone who reminded me of her. Hearing this same story, for the gazillionth time Syd said, "How long can you hold onto that? Can't you just let it go already?" It wasn't that I didn't want to let go—I just didn't know how. Later, when we were doing the mirroring process we learned at *Getting the Love You Want*, I discovered that the trigger for my anger was from a piece of unhealed baggage with my mother. Syd and I had several intense sessions about it that allowed me to work through my deep-rooted feelings of abandonment. Such issues are like weeds; they clutter up your life. Some can be pulled out without much effort. But then there are others with roots that go very deep; removing them can be quite a challenge. This was one of those, and I had been *schlepping* it around for years.

As I began finding myself, I became more independent, more open and confident. That was the good news. The bad news was worrying how all the changes taking place in me would affect my relationship with Syd. Thankfully, as he began opening to his own process, if anything we became closer and more connected than before. But I didn't know that then; back then I thought there was a real possibility we might not make it. Even so I had to keep moving forward, staying where I was just wasn't an option. And so, I went. There were times I lost my way, times I moved at a snail's pace, and times I forged ahead.

I always had this image of myself as being open-minded, nonjudgmental, and positive. But when I began to see that wasn't always so, I wasn't sure what to do with that information. And considering the possibility that I could actually be very negative, judgmental, and critical at times was out of the question; it didn't match up with the image. So I'd project my negative qualities where they were easy to see—onto other people. What I've learned about projection is that the qualities we love in other people are the qualities we love in ourselves. That resonated with me, until I heard the flip side. The qualities we can't stand in other people are the qualities we can't stand in ourselves. That resonated too, but I didn't like it much, even though instinctively I knew it was true.

That's where denial comes in (isn't it grand?). Up went a mask to keep those unpleasant qualities hidden from me. With my mask in place, I could paint a picture of everything in my life (including me) being just fine and dandy—even when it wasn't.

But once I began this journey, that all changed. Because suddenly, I had no more answers, now I had only questions, and I could no longer keep up the façade that everything was fine, not anymore. As I continued becoming more and more conscious, finally what I came to realize in time was that it wasn't *why* I needed to be asking; it was *how*. How did I need to change so I could accept my son and live my life more authentically?

When Don, a man in his mid-forties in the throes of depression, came to see me for counseling, he was filled with questions that he had no answers to. On the surface, Don had all the trappings of success, with what seemed like an ideal life as a successful accountant. As he began waking up, his life he discovered was not what it seemed.

Don's childhood dream had been to be a professional golfer. But his father, who was a salesman, never believed that his son could make a living as a golf pro and pushed him to give up what he saw as a childish fantasy. "Stop wasting your life on such foolishness," his father had told him time after time. "Become an accountant. That's an honorable profession. People will respect you and you'll always make a good living."

Don's father meant well. He wanted what was best for his son and thought he knew what that was, but truth be told, he had his own agenda; he was the one who had wanted to be an accountant but lacked the opportunity.

Living in denial, for years Don pushed aside his regrets about his lost golf career. But, as regrets are wont to do, they kept whispering in his ear, a little louder each time, until he couldn't ignore them any more. As he came out of denial, it was shattering for him to realize that because he hadn't listened to his own inner voice that the dream he had followed was his father's, not his own. In therapy he grieved for the loss of it.

As we explored the whys and wherefores of Don's career choice, the picture became more complex. Not only had Don given up his dream of being a golf pro to please his father, but his father had also given up the dream he had of being an accountant and became a salesman to please *his* father. Paradoxically, Don's father would brag that at least there was one accountant in the family; too bad it was the wrong one. What a tangled web family patterns weave! Both father and son ended up with jobs they hated, and a legacy of lost opportunity and regret.

And, since family patterns tend to repeat themselves, it didn't surprise me to learn that the intergenerational dynamics didn't end there. Don had a son of his own, who he had been coaching at golf; a sport the boy was good at but didn't have much interest in. Once Don saw how this pattern was affecting yet another generation, he stopped pushing golf and instead encouraged his son to follow his own dream: writing music and playing the guitar. For most of us waking from denial can be pretty painful, but as Don put it; it beats going through life half asleep. Don was able to make peace with his anger toward his father, while mine, toward my mother was still festering.

That's when I heard Malachy McCort's quote about resentment, and how it resonated. "Holding onto old resentments and toxic events is like taking poison and waiting for the other person to die." Intellectually I knew that holding onto my anger at my mother wasn't doing me any good, accepting it on an emotional level, though, that was a whole other story. But when I read *The Way* by Michael Berg—I got it. Berg shares the wisdom of Kabbalah through metaphor and story in a brilliantly understandable way that opened my heart to the realization that sure, my parents made more than their fair share of mistakes raising me, and I didn't get everything I needed from them, but then, who does? Parents can only give us what they have. The rest we have to get for ourselves. It was toward the end of her life, that my mother shared some of the stories that I had never heard before of her own difficult, and often traumatic childhood, and how she wished she had been less demanding, and more patient with my sister and me. When I had the realization that I could have said the same to my own children, what a sobering thought that was.

Like most other families, mine had their share of *mishagas* that in today's world would be called dysfunctional. Their unhealthy patterns kept on getting passed down from one generation, to the next generation, to the next. It wasn't possible for me to change what happened in the past, but what I could change was to stop those patterns from going any further. I've been working on that ever since.

So, after years of holding on—for dear life—to what I considered justified anger, finally I let that boomerang go, and this time, it didn't come back. It was gone—what a relief to let it go. I suppose one of the things that stopped me from letting go before was the fear that forgiving my mother would invalidate the pain she had caused me, and make it all okay. But I came to see that much of her behavior really wasn't even about me. It came from her history, from the template of how her parents had treated her, and how she in turn, then treated me. It was what she knew to do, and I don't think she ever even thought that there might be a different way.

There's a Buddhist story I heard of a man who comes to the edge of a river. He has to get to the other side, but can't find a way to get across. So he takes grasses, sticks, branches, and reeds and carefully lashes them together to make a raft. When it's done he paddles across the river and is so grateful when he gets to the other side. But once there, he doesn't know what to do with the raft. Should he tie it on the riverbank, so someone else might use it, or just let it float down the river? But he finds he can't part with it, so he carries the raft with him—for the rest of his life. So it is with the story of our lives—certain things have usefulness up to a point, but to carry them on our back for the rest of our lives becomes a burden.

So after years of blaming her, ultimately I was able to accept that my mother was the way she was for a reason, the *mishagas* didn't come out of nowhere. I didn't need to carry the pain of our relationship on my back any longer. I could set it down and remember the positive things I loved about her. Like how she loved being surrounded with family and friends; our house was the place everyone seemed to congregate when I was growing up. My mother loved to bake and our freezer was filled with delicious homemade pastries that she'd serve to whoever dropped by. Every week we went to the library together, and the two of us checked out so many books; walking home our arms would groan under the weight of them. My mother was a voracious reader: I don't think she was ever without a book to read by her nightstand. When she read a biography of Juan and Eva Peron, she was intrigued by their story; and read every book she could find about them in our neighborhood library.

No one I've ever known appreciated the beauty in nature or loved Mother Earth more than my mother. Just seeing a deer running in the woods was enough to send her into raptures. Here's one of my favorite stories. When I was about eight years old, a robin built a nest on our bathroom window ledge and laid four of the most beautiful blue eggs in it. Mom and I watched over them while waiting for the baby birds to hatch. When they did, we left birdseed for the mother. I was so excited; I went to the neighborhood hardware store and bought a fifty-pound bag of bird-seed (a little more than was needed for one small robin), that I *schlepped* home by myself—I wanted to make sure the robin had enough to eat. A precursor of things to come—when company's coming—better to have a little extra than not enough. For the past ten years each spring wrens have been making a nest in my mailbox, and then laying their tiny eggs there. It's such a thrill to see the baby birds. I always think of how excited Mom would have been to see them too.

In the face of many illnesses, my mother kept on going, always doing the best she could. She had great tenacity. In spite of having multiple sclerosis and being in a wheelchair, she would drive to the "Y" in a car that was specially fitted with hand controls, so she could go swimming. There were few things she loved more. When she was given a special shirt for swimming one hundred miles, she couldn't have been prouder if she had won an Olympic gold medal. I always got a kick out of hearing my mother *kvell* with delight to whoever had good news to share, whether it was a friend, family member, or even an acquaintance. She would genuinely be happy to hear about their good fortune. These days the anger is gone, and it's the good memories that I hold on to and cherish from my mother.

It was after that night at the movies, when I sat through *The Untouchables* (but saw very little of it), that I began paying attention to my life and my relationships. Once I did, the depression that had overwhelmed me after Michael came out dissipated. When weighing some of the positive and negative experiences of my life, as strange as it may sound, the depression came out on the positive side. It arrived like a knock on the door of my soul saying, "Enid, it's time to wake up now. This isn't what you came here for—something's not right—time to figure things out."

I wasn't sick, I was depressed, and no pill would have cured what ailed me. What I needed was to stay open to my grief and feel my way through it. I view the depression as the catalyst that woke me up, and led me onto a path toward wholeness.

After a few years had passed I saw *The Untouchables* again. I could hardly believe that my denial about my mother, and our relationship, could have lifted at that point in the movie with all that violence going on. Hard to figure how that happens.

It had become clear that Michael's coming out was more than just an opportunity for me to wake up. It was an incredible gift—one that was hard for me to see, hiding under all those layers of crap covering it, each layer had to be removed before that could happen. Sometimes I wonder what I would be doing today if Michael hadn't come out. Would I have ever realized that I had been living so unconsciously? Honestly, I don't think so. I was so totally oblivious that it took nothing less than the unraveling of my life to rouse me from my unconscious stupor. If it hadn't I'd probably still be stuck, going through the motions, not knowing I was only playing a role in someone else's script of my life.

But gratefully, I did wake up, and just in time to say adieu to the first half of my life and begin living the second half. The Russian poet Boris Pasternak said, "When a great moment knocks on the door of your life, very often it is no louder than the beating of your heart." Michael's coming out was such a moment for me, though it was more like a loud pounding than a knock. Thankfully I answered it and went about the process of discovering myself.

That summer night, over twenty-two years ago, when the narrow box I was living in collapsed, unwittingly I plunged into the sea of blame, guilt, and "if only"s that most parents go through. I tried to make sense of the news that I had a gay child. But I couldn't understand what went wrong, why was my child gay? First I blamed myself, then, I blamed Michael. Someone had to be blamed, didn't they? Isn't that what we're raised to believe? What I came to see was that much of the turmoil I was feeling wasn't even about Michael. He wasn't the one who needed fixing—I was.

Once upon (what feels like) a lifetime ago, I remember saying, with a good deal of hopelessness, that my life would never again be the same. I was right about that. Today my life is so much more than I ever dreamed it could be. I am so not the same woman I was back then. I hardly recognize her at all, the consummate people pleaser, always wanting to make the "right" impression. In those days I cared more about what other people thought than what I thought myself, and I let myself be treated like a *schmatah* (an old rag) by people who were only too happy to clean up the floor with me. If there was such a thing as having a disease to please, I had it for sure. Recently I've discovered a book for people pleasers, *The Disease to Please* by Harriet Braiker. I wish it had been available twenty years ago. It's one of the books I often recommend to clients who are pleasers.

Today I no longer do what other people think I'm supposed to do—just because they think I'm supposed to—at least most of the time. I have boundaries now and have learned to say no—Oy, was that hard to do! I've learned that living for myself is not selfish—who else should I live for? And now I know that when I speak my truth, other people will have their own opinions; they're entitled to theirs, but so am I, and their opinions have nothing to do with me. I've learned that the glue that holds families together is love and kindness—not guilt or fear. I wish my parents could have known that one. Getting to this place has taken me decades, but how long it took or how hard it was to get here isn't what matters. What matters is—I made it—this far, grateful to be living, not just surviving, knowing the difference between the two.

I had a lot of help along the way. Unexpectedly I found teachers, mentors, and friends offering help and support. People who understood, who I could trust, who were educated, tolerant, and compassion-ate, people who accepted me and my family for who we were, without any need for justification. Some of my most important mentors were found between the pages of books, like Louise Hay. Her book *You Can Heal Your Life* was the first self-help book I read. What a good one to start with. Her words helped me see the world in a different way. As I read her story, I realized I could choose to focus on what was posi-tive. I didn't have to hold onto my deeply ingrained negativity. What a concept. Who knew? Not me. But I was learning. Then I listened to *Pulling Your Own Strings* by Wayne Dyer, and learned I didn't have to be a victim; that too was a choice. While exploring Buddhism, I heard some of Jack Kornfield's tapes. His words were like a soothing balm. Finding com-passion for myself and others, I learned wouldn't be a one-time trip. It was one I would have to take again and again.

I heard Marianne Williamson speak at a Body & Soul Conference in Boston. I still have my notes from her session when she said, "If you empty out the pain, the wounding becomes the womb where you give birth." So it was for me when I was able to accept my son, I gave birth to a whole new life.

Then along came John Bradshaw, just at the time I was becoming aware of family systems. On Bradshaw's TV show, *The Family,* I saw a fascinat-ing example of how quickly a family can spin out of balance. Bradshaw had a large mobile sitting center stage with a mom and dad on either side of the first tier, a son and daughter on either side of the next tier, and on each side of the bottom tier, was a dog and cat. Bradshaw used the mobile to show how each part of the family was both independent, and also completely dependent on the other. The mobile family was balanced and in homeostasis until Bradshaw nudged the dad, saying, "Let's see what happens when dad comes home after a bad day at the office."

I watched as everyone on the mobile started swinging, and the whole family, dad, mom, brother, sister, even the pets became unstable. Eventually things settled down and the mobile family regained equilibrium. Visually, the demonstration showed how what affects one person in a family affects everyone in the family. That stuck in my mind because it showed me how out of control our family had been when Michael first came out. If that's the way it was even when dealing with something as minor as a rough day at work, it wasn't hard to imagine the upheaval that might take place during really hard times.

There were other teachers too, like Rosa Parks, one of my personal heroes. Back in 1955, I was a young girl when she helped change history in Montgomery, Alabama. On her way home from a long day's work, a bus driver asked Mrs. Parks to give up her seat so a white person could sit down; she refused. She was physically tired that night, but more than that, she was soul tired of being treated like a second-class citizen because of the color of her skin. Her courage sparked the Civil Rights Movement. She spoke for a whole people when she refused to get up. Her message was, "no more, enough, I will not be treated this way anymore." Rosa Parks taught me about having the courage to stand up for what's right, even when it goes against public opinion. Whenever I go to speak I bring her spirit with me.

Their words and the words of so many others seemed to find their way to me at the perfect time to teach me something I needed to know. Not all my teachers were positive; I had my share of negative ones too, but I learned from them all.

Over time Syd and I and our children have learned to communicate in healthier ways; we've gotten much better at it, at least most of the time—that too is a process. Our definition of family may have changed, but not our love for each other.

What I know now is that each of us has our own journey to take, so that we can learn whatever life lessons we need to learn. No matter how much I love my children or want to protect them from mishaps or roadblocks along the way, I can't give them my roadmap for their journey. They'll have to find their own way—and their own map to guide them.

CHAPTER 17

THE REST OF THE STORY
FROM MICHAEL

...of all mines of treasure,
one's own is the last to be dug up.
(Friedrich Nietzche)

ɘ

My mother often asks people when they first realized they were gay. For me, it was when I started going through puberty in the sixth grade. Like anyone at that age, I started experiencing sexual awakenings, but the object of my desire was boys—not girls. Those feelings continued growing stronger, and I honestly believed that I would die with my desires locked deep inside. Being gay was not an option. I WAS NOT GAY. To me, gay meant freak. The only person *I thought* might be gay was a very effeminate classmate who was constantly made fun of and ridiculed in the hallways. I avoided him like the plague to make sure I was never even seen in his presence. It would be many years before I would be able to use the word "gay" to describe myself.

In 1985, the summer before my senior year in college, I went abroad to study at Hebrew University in Jerusalem. On my way home, I had a three-day stopover in Paris.

Paris! I have the best coming out story EVER. I was alone on the Metro and an adorable blond guy came over and started talking with me. Now, keep in mind, Stacey, my girlfriend back at school, and I were both thinking of how and when I was going to propose, so my thoughts were far from sexual. He asked where I was staying, and when I told him the name of the hotel, he said there was a great gay bar right near there and would I like to go tonight. It must have been the look of shock or confusion on my face that prompted his asking "are you gay?" I vehemently shook my head no, while the word "yes" came out of my mouth. "Oh, you're confused," he said as I smiled and shrugged. He said he would pick me up at eleven p.m. in front of my hotel.

The only reason I agreed to go was that I felt it was a pretty safe bet I wouldn't run into anyone I knew halfway across the world. When I got off the Metro my heart was pounding! He picked me up and took me to my first gay bar in the heart of the Marais section of Paris. "You Spin Me Around" by Dead or Alive was *the* song that evening. We spent the next few days together, and my world was certainly spun around and around. When I returned to school, I couldn't go back to my former life. I met some wonderful gay friends and started facing the fact that there was no turning back.

Stacey was the first person I ever told. Telling her was horrifying, surreal and liberating all at the same time. Since she was relieved that I wasn't telling her that I was in love with another woman, at first she seemed to take it pretty well. But as the reality of this news sunk in, she became depressed, confused and very sad. In spite of this, today she is still one of my best friends and closest allies in the world.

Once I was able to tell Stacey and some other friends in college, I became bolder. But how would my parents take the news?? This was pre-Ellen coming out; pre-*Will and Grace* and pre-Rosie, and I was of course the ONLY gay person in Orlando, after all. I wanted to tell my parents, but friends were saying, "if you tell your parents...be prepared to lose them." We were such a close-knit family; I just couldn't imagine them turning their back on me.

Over the course of that year, I made the decision to live the life I was meant to live and I wanted the people important to me to know. At the top of that list were my mom and dad. Some friends chose not to confide in their parents, keeping their sexual orientation off limits. But I saw them drift farther and farther away from their parents. That just wasn't an option for me. I knew my parents would be unhappy, but I had faith that they would ultimately come around, and in the summer of 1986, we had "the talk."

My mom had an immediate, visceral reaction. She couldn't even look me in the eyes. She lashed out frequently. I was able to handle most of the barrage, but there was one outburst I wasn't prepared for. At that point in my life, I was keeping kosher and very connected to my Jewish roots. That changed in an instant when she temporarily morphed into her own mother saying, "And you call yourself a Jew."

Like most of the Jewish people I knew, I was taught to believe that gays and Jews were like oil and vinegar: they don't mix terribly well. A cliché, but a truism if ever there was one. I couldn't reconcile that, so I stopped keeping kosher and essentially started to abandon all things Jewish. Over those first weeks my mother's get-him-out-of-the-house energy was palpable. If she wasn't trying to convince me that I was throwing my life away, she was crying in her bedroom. If my father would have let her, I think she would have thrown me out of the house. My father remained loving, but he wasn't able to accept me either, and kept coming up with ways to "fix" me. It was clear we had a long way to go.

The next few years were the hardest. It went from, "Michael's coming home! Michael's coming home!" to, "O-h...M-y...G-o-d, Michael's coming home." That was the worst part for me. I had been brought up to feel confident, totally worthy, full of self-esteem and special, but all that came crashing down. Those attributes were reserved for the old Michael, version1: straight. Now I was Michael, version 2: gay.

Through a decade of subsequent therapy, weekend seminars and personal growth courses like *UYO* (Understanding Yourself and Others) and *The Experience*, I reclaimed that man who was once the old Michael. But I also learned that suppressing all those feelings during those formative, early years can have a powerful impact. For me, this was especially true when choosing a career path.

I had started producing theater at the age of ten when I created the Kewanee Street Players doing *Robin Hood* with the other neighborhood kids.

Later, in college I legitimately produced, conducted, acted and directed with the musical theater group on campus, all while studying for exams in organic chemistry for my pre-med major! After taking an elective Theater Administration class and loving it, I thought about studying theater arts or becoming a director or producer.

What? Are you kidding? No, Jewish boys from Orlando don't do that. They become doctors. So I maintained my pre-med path and applied to medical school. I remember that pivotal day when the rejection letter arrived. Was this divine intervention telling me to explore other avenues? Of course not....I'd apply to my second choice. I got accepted, worked hard for my degree, internship, and residency, and went on to become a physician. Why didn't I have the courage to follow my passions at that time? More therapy required.

It was years later, during my UYO course, that I learned why. *That* issue ran deep. My mom had gone through the UYO program, and I was impressed with her dramatic transformation, so I agreed to go as well. We were doing some role-playing and anger work. The instructor asked me to get angry at my father.

"I love my father," I replied.

"Of course you love your father," she said, "but you're also really angry at him."

I went through the motions of playing angry, but it wasn't real. I really do love my dad, and I had a pretty uneventful, privileged childhood. Then the instructor asked me to select someone in the class who looked like my dad. I picked John, the closest facsimile I could find, who got in my face and started yelling at me. Additional, but less convincing going-through-the-motions of playing angry followed, until he said something that stopped me in my tracks and opened the flood gates.

"Cut the crap, Michael" he said, as my father, "I gave you everything and you disappointed me. You turned out to be a fucking faggot."

It was as if I were slapped in the face. My sexual orientation had not come up in this class and I was stunned. Then I started to cry; the kind of cry usually only done once in your life: the guttural kind.

The instructor told me, "Now turn the tears to anger."

I became enraged. They needed four large men to hold me back. After the exercise when everyone in the room had calmed down, she told me to sit on "my dad's" lap and complete this sentence…"Daddy, all I ever wanted was…"

It's amazing how we all long for our parent's acceptance—for who, what, and how we are. I knew at an early age (twelve to be exact) that I was different and that society had a very specific perspective on my kind of different. I was not going to be accepted. Specifically, my father was not going to accept me.

What profession would command respect from society and ultimately my father? Well, he's an attorney, so I have to one-up that: medicine. I became a physician because I believed that whatever else happened in my personal life, society (and my father) would have to respect me if I were a doctor. I subconsciously chose a career path that would take decades of my life because working in the arts would enhance the stereotype and prevent that acceptance. Ironically, unlike my mom's client who dreamed of being a professional golfer only to have his dreams squashed by his father, my parents both encouraged me to do whatever I wanted to do, never putting outward pressure on me to become a doctor. That war was an internal one as I battled the perceptions of what I believed was expected of me.

But it's important to note that, as I write this, I am no longer practicing medicine. Instead I am producing theater, opera and developing entertainment projects in Southern California, my real life's work. My "second half of life."

The next chapter for me is figuring out how to bring Judaism back into my life. I'd like to be able to find a place where being Jewish and gay are not mutually exclusive. Shawn and I started going to the gay and lesbian synagogue in New York when we were preparing for our commitment ceremony in 1995, but the gay rabbi was distant because we were an "interfaith" gay couple. That was the last straw for me. For years, we basically lost any spiritual or religious connection to the world. But this year I went to High Holiday services for the first time in many years and really enjoyed it. There was a pamphlet on the table outside the sanctuary about welcoming gay and lesbian Jews! Things seemed to have changed a bit, so maybe Shawn and I are ready to give it another try.

Even though it has been one hell of a ride, I don't regret any of it. It may have taken a long time to get where I am today, but it's been well worth the trip. My relationship with my parents and the rest of my family is close and loving, and truly I feel blessed by their unconditional acceptance.

I am especially happy that Shawn got to meet my grandmother before she died because she was actually responsible for our meeting. She had taken our entire family on a cruise earlier that year where I met Shawn. When I did come out to her, she was curious to know whether I was seeing anyone. When I said yes, she asked if it was "that cute blond from the ship?" I was floored. The next time we were in Miami, Shawn and I took her out for dinner. It was a joyous evening filled with probing questions, laughter and cracking shellfish (I'm obviously no longer keeping kosher). That night ended up being the last time we were together. I am so thankful I was able to really share my life with her for the first time and do so in the presence of my future life partner. It was a magic night indeed.

A few years ago Shawn and I were watching the shocking season premier of *Queer as Folk* on Showtime. "My parents are at home watching this," I said. "GOOD GOD!" While they are completely transformed at this point, and comfortable representing all parents worldwide in any gay cause...gay SEX is another story. Still something we don't discuss around the dinner table. But then again...would we really want to??

EPILOGUE

We do not succeed in changing things
according to our desire,
but gradually our desire changes.
The situation that we hoped to change
because it was intolerable
becomes unimportant.
We have not managed to surmount the obstacle,
as we were absolutely determined to do,
but life has taken us around it,
led us past it,
and then if we turn around
to gaze at the remote past,
we can barely catch sight of it,
so imperceptable has it become.
(Marcel Proust)

A few weeks after I read Michael's chapter, "The Rest of the Story," a young lesbian woman came to see me for counseling, making the timing of her session like a giant exclamation point. Since discovering she was gay when she was fourteen, Sherri had been hiding the truth from her parents. Now, eleven years later, what she wanted was to end "the game" she was playing with her parents, that like them, she too was waiting for Mr. Right to come along and sweep her off her feet. "That's their dream," she said, "not mine." She was dreaming of Ms. Right.

Sherrie knew she couldn't hide the truth from her parents forever, at some point they would have to know she was gay. But she also knew there would be high drama involved when her parents found out and she wasn't sure she was ready to deal with it. Sherri's parents were expecting, as she put it, the whole enchilada: the big splashy wedding, the handsome groom, and the grandchildren. Having a lesbian daughter wasn't part of their plan. Round and round she went with all the reasons she should tell her parents, and all the reasons she shouldn't, making herself a wreck in the process.

Sherri was stuck, vacillating between wanting her parents to know, and fearing what would happen if they did, a familiar place for so many gays. She knew the possibility was very real that they could cut her out of their lives entirely. "I think the worst part for me," she said, "is I won't be their pride and joy anymore."

Hearing her words, it was like déjà vu, and I felt the universality of her dilemma. Being caught in that place of limbo trying to make the decision to come out, was not only her fear, but also at one time or another, the fear of countless other gay children, including my own son.

"My parents are wonderful people in many ways," Sherri said. "But they're homophobic people too. Is it worth the risk to tell them, if I lose their love? If only my mother could be like you," she added.

I smiled at the irony and told her I was a very different person when my son came out, nothing like I am now—not at all accepting. But that for me, after all the upheaval, the ending turned out to be a whole lot better than the beginning. My son's coming out turned out to be the catalyst for my growth, maybe the same would be true for her parents. But after weighing the situation, Sherri felt she had too much to lose and thoughts of telling her parents have remained at status quo for now. Coming out is risky business. There are no guarantees for a happy ending.

A time most parents don't forget is when their child comes out. Syd and I are no exception. The night Michael first told us he was gay is forever etched in my memory, for many reasons. But something about it I barely noticed that night was that for a brief moment in time, I imagined our family in the future, the four of us sitting around our kitchen table like we had so many times in the past. I saw us there enjoying each other's company, lightheartedly talking about the day's happenings—and all was well. Also I had this sense that having survived the turmoil about to come, we were more deeply connected to each other. That picture would pop into my mind, just for a moment during some of the worst of times. Years later I realized this wasn't the first time I saw myself in the future, visualizing a good ending. Once when I was in graduate school I was feeling like I couldn't sit through one more class, or take one more test. I was thinking about dropping out when I saw myself walking across a stage, in my cap and gown to collect my diploma feeling an incredible sense of validation at having reached my goal. I believe mentally picturing that scene, happening in the future, helped me to get there.

A few years ago, I was at a seminar with Bill O'Hanlon, author of *Do One Thing Different,* when he told the most poignant story. O'Hanlon was at an international therapy conference where the guest speaker was Viktor Frankl, author of *Man's Search for Meaning,* the story of how Frankl not only survived but kept hope alive during the Holocaust. As Austrian Jews, Frankl and his family watched the rise of Hitler in Germany and knew it was only a matter of time before the Nazi invasion would begin. If they didn't leave, their lives would be in peril. One sister escaped, but Frankl refused to leave, knowing his elderly parents couldn't survive on their own. So he, his pregnant wife, and his brother stayed behind in Vienna to look after them.

When the Nazis came, Frankl and his family were sent first to Theresienstadt concentration camp. Then they were separated and were deported to other camps including Bergen-Belsen and Auschwitz, where one by one his parents, wife, and brother all perished. It was at Auschwitz that the manuscript of his book—his life's work—was discovered, hidden in the lining of his coat, and destroyed. Painstakingly Frankl reconstructed his manuscript, first in his mind, then on slips of stolen paper. His desire to complete his book kept him alive through his devastating ordeal.

Toward the end of the war, prisoners in the camp saw British and American planes flying overhead more frequently, and knew the war would soon be over. But so did many of the Nazis, who emptied out the camps and began marching the survivors for days and weeks, and some even months. One day on such a march Frankl, suffering with typhus, fell and could not find the strength to get up. A guard began beating him and shouted, "get up, or I'll shoot you." After all he had been through Frankl could not physically pick himself up. But then, he pictured himself in the future, standing at a podium, giving a speech to a roomful of people. From what was for him the hopeless present, Frankl was not able to get up. But by seeing himself in the future, having survived his ordeal, somehow he found the strength to get up and keep marching. Days later he was liberated.

After the war, Frankl became a world-renowned psychiatrist. And the future he pictured became a reality some years later when there he stood at a podium, in front of thousands of therapists at an international psychotherapy conference. He was giving the keynote address, and told this story to thunderous applause. What an unforgettable story of what a person is capable of overcoming. Since Frankl's death, his book has inspired millions and has sold more than ten million copies.

When I heard O'Hanlon tell this profound story, I thought about the value of looking into the future, creating a better ending there, and moving toward it. It reminded me of a quote from one of my mentors, Dr. Bob Bollet, who said, "No one can go back and make a brand new start, but anyone can start now, and make a brand new ending." I believe the vision of my family together and whole, helped lead me to where I am today in spite of all the twists and turns I took along the way.

In January of 2008 Syd and I did an interview for StoryCorp, a National nonprofit oral history project whose mission is to honor and celebrate one another's lives, by capturing the stories of ordinary people. Our conversation was recorded and has been archived at the Library of Congress in Washington, DC. We felt if by publicly telling the story of Michael's coming out, we could help one other parent find a place of acceptance with their gay child—it would make it worthwhile. To Syd's and my surprise, a five-minute piece from our thirty-five minute interview was selected to air on WMFE (National Public Radio) in Orlando. The producer of our piece, Katie Ball, did an amazing job, capturing the essence of what we wanted to convey. Others who heard it agreed. I gave a copy of the CD to a friend who didn't catch the interview on the radio. After she heard it, she asked if she could share it with a woman she knew who hadn't spoken to her lesbian daughter for over twelve years. Of course I said yes.

When my friend played the CD of our full interview to Julia, she wasn't a bit interested in hearing it, and at first listened half-heartedly. But as the interview went on, Julia began listening more thoughtfully. She understood our story—it was also very much her own. The tears came and something opened in her. She thought of her daughter—her only daughter—and of the separation between them that had become unbearable. She thought about the anger and the shame she had been harboring for so many years. What had it gotten her, if in the end she lost her child? After sleeping on it, Julia took the first step; she picked up the phone and called her daughter. Since they've reconnected, they speak to each other often. They have a lot of catching up to do—twelve years of it. This past Christmas Julia visited her daughter and met her daughter's partner for the first time, a stretch for her, but that part takes time, and she's working on it. Julia opened a door. Behind it, waiting on the other side, she found her daughter. Knowing that our story helped one family in such a profound way not only warmed our hearts, it made our story so worth the telling.

So much has changed for me since that faraway summer of what would come to be my awakening. My dream of becoming a therapist, once seemingly unreachable, is now a reality. The work I do is incredibly gratifying, and since I could have been the poster mom for the "unaccepting parent," working with gay people coming out, or their parents, feels like a perfect fit. Even though I'm a million miles away from the coming-out part of the journey—I still remember how it feels.

Today I'm mindful that like the Talmudic tale from this book's title, Michael too had moved to a distant kingdom, one that was strange and relatively unfamiliar to us. Even though Syd and I viewed this new terrain with aversion, shame, and a sizable share of ignorance, Michael remained loving and respectful. He understood our struggle and gave us time to become accustomed to this new kingdom, a place we never expected to find ourselves. He put up with our self-absorbed view of how his sexual orientation affected us, and was patient in spite of the fact that we were so wrapped up in our own journey that we had barely considered his. He was encouraging as we traveled at a snail's pace, going inch by inch until we came to a place of acceptance. But early on

Michael let us know he had come as far as he could. As much as he loved us, and wanted us to be a part of his life, he would not deny his authentic self, hiding in a closet pretending to be someone he was not. He had to live his own life. For Syd and me, figuring it all out took a lot longer; this book is a testament to that. But, thankfully, we came to a place of understanding, and when we did, we knew it was we, and not Michael who were the ones who had to change. It was up to us to travel the rest of the way.

ACKNOWLEDGMENTS

With the help of many people this book came into being. First and foremost I want to thank my beloved husband Syd for reading and listening to revision after revision with infinite patience. His constant love and acceptance has been the catalyst that allowed me to inch forward as I worked through my many issues.

My love and gratitude to my son Michael for trusting that Syd and I would work through our homophobia and come to a place of acceptance. The courage and love he showed in coming out is what brought about this spiritual journey. To my son Howard, my love and heartfelt appreciation not only for his support, but also for the depth of his compassion, especially during some of the most difficult days. With thanks to my daughter-in-law Liz, who was there with an open heart for Michael and for me from the beginning, and for my son-in-law Shawn for his love and understanding. I hold each of them always in my heart.

Deepest thanks go to Louise Sheehy, Rick Stone, Adele Azar-Ruquoi, Dawn Lipthrott, Maria Boudet, Elizabeth Cohen, and Lynn Schiffhorst, for their ongoing love and support. Also thanks to Jay Brophy, Howard Axner, Chris Alexander-Manley, and Tommy Manley for their help and encouragement, and to my loving circle of friends who shared their wisdom and understanding.

And of course my profound gratitude for the invaluable counsel of Hedy Schleifer, Bob Bollet, and Pete Fischer. Their loving hearts and outstretched hands helped Syd and me find our way.

Many thanks to Tom Dyer for his continuing support, and for giving me the opportunity to begin honing my writing skills in a monthly column written with Syd for the *Watermark,* Central Florida's gay newspaper.

With love and appreciation to my dear friend Steven Cooper, author, Emmy-winning journalist, and teacher extraordinaire. His insight and vision helped me find my voice and brought me to the next level.

And deepest appreciation goes to Elsa Peterson, whose editing skills were invaluable. Her honesty in editing the final versions of the book—was sometimes difficult to hear—but oh so necessary.

I want to especially thank the guardian angel of this project, my dear friend, Jerry Schiffhorst, a professor of English and author. His belief in my story urged me on to finally complete this memoir. My deepest appreciation to him for his encouragement and for lovingly editing the early versions of the book.

ACKNOWLEDGMENTS

In memory of my mother Betty Cohen Duchin, a teacher of many lessons, and my father Herman Duchin whose light and love are always with me.

All of those authors listed in the Resource section have been teachers who have helped illuminate the way for me as well.

With regard to any reference to clients, in certain instances some represent a composite of people, and all names have been changed.

Beattie, Melody. *Codependent No More* (Center City: Hazelden, 1987).

Berg, Michael. T*he Way: Using The Wisdom Of Kabbalah For Spiritual Transformation And Fulfillment* (Hoboken: John Wiley & Sons, Inc. 2001).

Blumenfeld, Warren. *Homophobia: How We All Pay The Price* (Boston: Beacon Press 1992).

Bradshaw, John. *Bradshaw On: The Family* (Deerfield Beach: Health Communications, Inc., 1996).

Braiker, Harriet. *The Disease To Please: Curing The People Pleasing Syndrome* (New York: McGraw-Hill, 2001).

Dyer, Wayne. *Pulling Your Own Strings* (New York: Crowell Company, 1978).

Eichberg, Rob. *Coming Out: An Act of Love* (New York; PLUME, The Penguin Group, 1991).

Frankl, Viktor. *Man's Search for Meaning*, (New York: Simon & Schuster, 1984).

Gomes, Peter. *The Good Book: Reading the Bible With Mind And Heart,* (New York: HarperCollins, 1996).

Hay, Louise. *You Can Heal Your Life* (Carlsbad, CA: Hay House, 1984).

Kornfeld, Jack. *After The Ecstasy, The Laundry: How The Heart Grows Wise on the Spiritual Path* (New York: Bantam Trade Paperback Edition, 2001).

_____*Meditation for Beginners* Audio CD.

Marcus, Eric. *Is It A Choice? Answers To The Most Frequently Asked Questions about Gay & Lesbian People* (New York: HarperCollins, 1993).

O'Hanlon, Bill. *Do One Thing Different* (New York: HarperCollins, 1999).

Pearson Carol Lynn. *Good-bye, I Love You* (New York: Random House, 1986).

Rosen, Sidney. *My Voice Will Go With You: The Teaching Tales of Milton Erickson* (New York: W.W. Norton & Company, Inc, 1991).

Schachter-Shalomi, Zalman. *From Age-ing to Sage-ing* (New York: Warner Books, 1995).

Schleifer, Hedy & Yumi Schleifer. *Crossing the Bridge*, DVD, www.hedyyumi.org

Spong, John Shelby. *Living in Sin?: A Bishop Rethinks Human Sexuality* (New York: HarperCollins Publishers, Inc.,1988).

Stone, Richard. *The Healing Art of Storytelling: A Sacred Journey of Personal Discovery* (Lincoln, NE: Author's Choice Press, 2004).

White, Mel. *Stranger at the Gate: To Be Gay and Christian in America* (New York: PLUME, The Penguin Group, 1995).

ORGANIZATIONS

American Civil Liberties Union (ACLU):

The ACLU's Lesbian & Gay Rights Project fights discrimination against LGBT people and families. www.aclu.org

Equality Florida:

A statewide education and advocacy organization dedicated to eliminating discrimination based on sexual orientation, race, gender and class. www.eqfl.org

Gay & Lesbian Alliance Against Defamation (GLAAD):

Dedicated to promoting and ensuring fair, accurate and inclusive representation of people and events in the media as a means of eliminating homophobia and discrimination based on gender identity and sexual orientation. www.glaad.org

Gay, Lesbian and Straight Educational Network (GLSEN):

A national education organization focused on ensuring safe schools for ALL students. www.glsen.org

Human Rights Campaign: (HRC)

A bipartisan organization that works to advance equality based on sexual orientation and gender expression and identity. www.hrc.org

Lambda Legal:

A national organization committed to achieving full recognition of the civil rights of lesbians, gay men, bisexuals, transgender people and those with HIV through impact litigation, education and public policy work. www.lambdalegal.org

National Gay & Lesbian Task Force:

The first national lesbian, gay, bisexual and transgender civil rights and advocacy organization, a leading voice for freedom, justice, and equality. www.thetaskforce.org

Parents, Family and Friends of Lesbians & Gays (PFLAG):

Promotes the health and well-being of gay, lesbian, bisexual and transgendered persons, their families and friends through support, education, and advocacy to end discrimination and to secure equal civil rights. PFLAG acts to create a society that is healthy and respectful of human diversity. www.pflag.org

<u>SoulForce</u>:

The purpose of Soulforce is freedom for lesbian, gay, bisexual, and transgender people from religious and political oppression through the practice of relentless nonviolent resistance. www.soulforce.org

Adventures in Intimacy (Hedy & Yumi Schleiffer).
www.hedyyumi.org

Getting the Love you Want www.gettingtheloveyou-
want.com

Speaking Out Against Homophobia (Warren Blumenfeld)

UYO (Understanding Yourself and Others)—now
called P3 (Personal Power and Prosperity) www.
personalpowerandprosperity.com

YIDDISH GLOSSARY

Buba—grandmother
Chupah—a temporary shelter Jewish couples traditionally stand under when saying their vows
Fagele—derogatory express for someone gay
Haimish—homey
Havurah—group of friends
Kaddish—mourner's prayer
Kvell–being delighted
Kvetch—complaining
Latkas—pancakes
Loshon Hora—gossiping in a derogatory way
Mazel Tov—good luck
Mensch—righteous person
Minyan—ten men who gather to say prayers
Mishagas—craziness
Mispucha—immediate and extended family
Mizinka—baby
Schlep—drag
Schmatah—an old rag
Shabbat—Jewish Sabbath
Shiva—Jewish mourning period
Shunda—disgrace
Zeda—grandfather

ABOUT THE AUTHOR

A few years after her son came out; Enid went back to school to become a psychotherapist. She now specializes in gay and lesbian issues. Knowing personally as well as professionally how painful the coming out process can be for both parents and children, she is dedicated to helping people examine their stereotypical misconceptions about homosexuality by bringing gay and lesbian issues out of the closet and into the mainstream. In *The Rest of the Way*, Enid draws on her life experiences to illustrate where the roots of prejudice and shame begin.

A longtime member of PFLAG (Parents, Family, and Friends of Lesbians and Gays), Enid has served on both the Orlando Board of Directors of GLBCC (Gay, Lesbian, and Bisexual Community Center), and on the Orlando Board of PFLAG for over ten years. For three years, she and her husband Syd wrote a column in *Watermark*, Central Florida's bi-monthly gay newspaper called, "A Parent's Perspective," to add their voices to the cause of gay acceptance. Enid and Syd live in Central Florida.

Visit Enid's website at:
www.restoftheway.com

For information about workshops or speaking
engagements contact Syd at:
Therestoftheway@aol.com
or
Rest of the Way
P. O. Box 940276
Maitland, FL 32794--0276